THE EUROPE CODE

GLOBAL POLITICS AND THE POSITIONING OF EUROPE

Who feels addressed

A conclusion of the findings
from the book
POLITICS @ GLOBAL-WORLD.INTL

CONTENT

KEY WORDS

Paradigm Shift - World Clusters - International Policy Excellence - Political Creativity - Global Challenges - Narrow Nationalism - Key Technologies - Toxic Politics - International Policy Co-Creation - Evidence-Based Approach - Advisory Agencies - Global Alliances - Skills Development - EU Weaknesses - Extremisms - Unqualified Political Leaders - European Axes - The Weimar Triangle - Global Governance - Deterrence - Authoritarian Regimes - False Political Information - Disinformation - Information Warfare - Sovereignty - Personnel Assessments in Politics - Historical Connections - Effective Communication - International Decisions - Political Charisma - Influencing World Politics - Professional Judgment - Culture of Responsibility - Informed Citizens - Humanistic European Values - European Macro-Regions - Populism and Nationalism - Defending the Free World - Clown Parties - Europe's Inner Unity - The European Project - Rational Management in Politics - International Congresses - Cognition and Decision-Making - International Sport - Economic Resilience - Cyberwarfare

A. PARADIGM SHIFT

We work a lot with emotions and that's a good thing, but if we overdo it, the whole structure would collapse on us. International politics is often complex and dynamic. Is it too much for the civil society? With so many different events and topics, it can be difficult to keep track. This can cause people to lose interest in politics. We all face never-ending tasks. Turning away from what is happening, tuning out and isolating oneself is neither a political nor a personal solution. We are simply a part of the overall development and cannot separate ourselves from it. Being consciously informed, this makes politics interesting in terms of current events and relevance. Both the past and present are moving, exhilarating and full of effects.

Who is responsible? The responsibility of society is as

great as we are all part of society. Why do we not prevent obvious negative developments together? Power structures, conflicts of interest, indifference, fear of consequences, lack of awareness of the issues, as well as insufficient resources and capacities are behind it. These challenges require a paradigm shift. There is a need for a collective commitment to deal with international and national political developments in an informed, committed and proactive manner. Only in this way can we better manage the complexities of our time and prevent negative outcomes in order to create an informed and more resilient society.

We'll just wing it! After all, why bother with the tedious task of understanding complex international issues when one can simply rely on sheer optimism and a dash of overconfidence? What could possibly go wrong when leaders choose to dismiss the intricacies of international relations? Perhaps they believe that global conflicts will resolve themselves, if only ignored long enough, or that economic sanctions are just friendly nudges rather than serious diplomatic tools.

It's almost touching how some people think that international politics is as easy as ordering a cup of coffee - just choose your favorite blend and hope for the best! One could almost admire the audacity of such an approach, if it weren't for the minor detail that reality has a pesky way of intruding. The complex web of alliances, historical grievances and economic interdependencies simply refuses to untangle itself on command. It seems that, despite the best efforts to sidestep reality, success in international politics stubbornly requires an understanding of and engagement with its inherent challenges.

International relations are essential when it comes to addressing issues of security, health, prosperity and social justice particularly on a global scale. It radiates to the smaller units above the globe. In an increasingly interconnected world, the actions of one country can have far-reaching consequences that impact the entire international community. This is why cooperation and collaboration among nations are essential in addressing these pressing challenges. In an era of heightened global threats such as terrorism, cyber attacks and nuclear proliferation, countries must work together to combat these threats and ensure the safety and security of their citizens. If the brutality of elbow strikes is the focus, something has gone wrong in social engagement.

How to escape the dilemma? With the existing potential, it should be possible to find answers. If war suddenly reappears on the doorstep of Europe's finally achieved peace, something in the prophylaxis must change. Above all, resistance must be offered. There is a constant showdown of the naughtiness of the political mind. Who or what is the enemy? Society is increasingly experiencing the effects of deliberately caused electrical power outages, blocking of infrastructure or paralysis of telecommunications. Psychological warfare is carried out in denial and cover-up. Politics must look closely and look ahead. Simulations of blatant defense have the disadvantage that they always lag behind. Forward-looking security policy will rely on designing deterrence proactively. The wrong lessons will inevitably lead to disaster. There is movement in the paralysis of fear. Health is another area in which international politics is needed. As health becomes more intertwined with foreign policy, security, development and trade, new diplomatic skills are needed to negotiate health priorities alongside other interests. Global pandemics have highlighted the need for countries to work together to address health emergencies and ensure access to healthcare for all. An intensive cooperation supports sustainable development by framing health as a social, economic and political issue.

Furthermore, international politics is essential in promoting economic prosperity and social justice. Issues such as trade agreements, development aid and climate change require coordinated action from countries around the world to ensure sustainable economic growth and reduce poverty and inequality. By facilitating coordinated action among countries, international politics addresses key issues that transcend national boundaries and require collective efforts to achieve sustainable development and equitable outcomes. Well-designed trade agreements can promote economic growth by opening up new markets, encouraging specialization, and fostering competition.

However, trade agreements must also consider the potential impact on vulnerable sectors and ensure that the benefits of trade are distributed fairly among all stakeholders. International development aid, provided by wealthier nations and multilateral organizations, aims to support economic and social progress in developing countries. This aid can take various forms, such as financial assistance, technical expertise, and capacity building.

Effective development aid helps to reduce poverty, improve access to education and healthcare, and promote sustainable development practices.
The effectiveness of future events of international cooperation depends on the willingness of states to look beyond national self-interest and pursue common goals. The rise of populism and the retreat of many countries into isolationist policies pose a serious threat to international cooperation. It is closely linked to the ability of states to adapt flexibly to new challenges and developments.

While the idea of ignoring difficulties in international

politics is an entertaining fantasy, it is perhaps best left to the realm of satire. For those tasked with navigating turbulent waters and clearly identifying challenges, this remains an indispensable part of the job - much to the chagrin of those who don't realize it. International politics is inherently complex and full of multi-layered issues. Balancing the competing interests requires negotiation and international cooperation. Ignoring or failing to recognize these challenges leads to ineffective decisions and strategies. Political decision-makers should therefore understand their own capabilities and limitations.

Overestimation of abilities due to lack of recognition of difficulties leads to poor outcomes. This implies that successful political action depends on a realistic and comprehensive understanding of the international landscape. To be successful in international politics the players have to understand the intricacies and difficulties of their profession. And the civil society has to control it.

This understanding enables the development of effective strategies that address the real problems. Essentially, success in international politics depends on a realistic evaluation of the challenges and the ability to address them effectively. The explosive cause of global problems today lies in the interconnectedness and interdependence of the global community. Local events can quickly have a global impact while maintaining the ability to be effective.

The concept of sovereignty and the role of society in shaping political developments stays at the center of events. Society, as a collective entity, holds the power to influence political decisions and outcomes. By joining interest groups and engaging in constructive dialogue, politicians work towards common goals and overcome divisive nationalist tendencies. This is especially important in a globalized world where cooperation and inclusivity are key to addressing common challenges.

Nationalist thinking, by its very nature, promotes an "us versus them" mentality. This perspective raisess suspicion and mistrust towards other nations or groups perceived as different or external. The consequences of this mindset can be wide-spread and damaging, both externally and internally. Nationalist thinking often leads to strained international relationships. Policies and rhetoric driven by nationalism result in conflicts, trade wars and a general breakdown in diplomatic relations. This isolates a country on the global stage and significantly limits opportunities for cooperation and mutual benefit. Nationalist ideologies fuel xenophobia and racism, as they tend to emphasize the superiority of one nation or group over others. This leads to discriminatory policies and social unrest.

We know this from so-called Trumpism, Qannon or the egalitarian groups.

The tendencies in the politics of Trump or Putin share some commonalities, such as the emphasis on national sovereignty, criticism of the global elite and the promotion of nationalist and patriotic sentiments. They are often associated with more authoritarian and populist approaches, which ignore facts and truths in favor of emotions and narratives. Trump's foreign policy is based on the principle of "America First", which means that the national interests of the United States are put ahead of global interests and the liberal world order. This approach is nationalist and isolationist. QAnon supporters in turn believe that Trump is fighting against the satanist elite that controls the USA. This elite is referred to as the "Deep State" and is portrayed by QAnon as a threat to national sovereignty and people's freedom. Putin's politics are not much different as they are characterized by a strongly nationalistic and brutally authoritarian orientation, which emphasizes only the importance of the own culture and the need to protect national sovereignty.

If mistakes made in Europe appear, the same can be said

on the other side of the Atlantic. If Donald Trump, the star of the american ultra-rights, propagates that all evil comes from Europe, China or the Middle East, it can be expected that Europe will have to react in its own interest and join his forces. The European continent must be confident that it can maintain equal distance from all sides to avoid being overwhelmed. For the rest of a long time, the incompetence and moral dubiousness of an American polit-clan influenced the world stage. Clintonomics plunged not only the American but also the international economy into a deep abyss. A late consequence was the unexpected election victory of Donald Trump 2016, largely seen as a reckoning with the dubious political clan, the Clintons. A tougher and, above all, fickle mentality is unexpectedly spreading on both the right and the left political flank of the USA, which can hopefully be stopped, but at least remains present in people's thoughts.

Within a nation, the emphasis on the narrow national thinking creates divisions between different groups. Ethnic, religious or cultural minorities may be viewed with suspicion or hostility, leading to social fragmentation and conflict. Nationalist rhetoric deepens political divisions. This suppresses political debate and leads to authoritarian tendencies. Because nationalist thinking fosters a climate of mistrust, it undermines the trust of citizens in each other. Encouraging people to look at others with suspicion undermines social cohesion and the sense of community.

Nationalist thinking leads generally to strict provincialism in politics. It is on the way to restricting international cooperation. This limits the exchange of ideas, talents and resources and hinders innovation and progress. The mere focus on preserving national identity leads to cultural stagnation. It's part of the false beauty of political divisions. The argument is: „Who needs democracy and a strong debate when you can have a good old authoritarian regime? Nothing makes the social fabric stronger than mistrust and paranoia. Imagine the strong sense of community, that comes from people constantly watching each other. Who needs innovation and progress when cultural stagnation can prevail?" A society that wants to avoid different perspectives and ideas, desperately merges into its own little bubble of outdated practices.

The negative impact of malicious nationalism on politics cannot be overlooked. It is politically irresponsible and unforgivable, when functioning systems collapse. The impact of such a collapse is wide-ranging, affecting not only the immediate socio-political environment, but also the long-term viability and prosperity of transnational communities. When forward-looking ideas fail, the momentum of progress is lost. This leads to stagnation in critical areas, such as technology, healthcare and education. Their collapse suppresses creativity and progress, prevents the development of new solutions. Conversely, forward-looking systems form the basis for innovations.

Identifying critical technologies means to determine the key technology sectors that are crucial for Europe's prosperity, security and global competitiveness. This should include not just commercial and dual-use technologies, but also those concerning critical raw materials, advanced materials, AI, biotechnology, quantum computing and other strategic areas. The European Union's policy approach must go beyond the traditional framework and become a "grand strategy" to create technological and industrial advantages.

Coordinated action in alliances creates an approach that is capable to countering external pressure. That aligns security, trade and research policies to create technological and industrial advantages. Functioning single systems under a common umbrella are crucial for supporting industries and jobs. Their collapse would lead to job losses and greater economic hardship for many people. It woud reduce confidence in the market, discourage investment and exacerbate economic downturns. The economic cooperation in a united Europe is an important pillar, but cannot stand alone. All aspects must be linked to other key areas such as collective security, finance and foreign policy. Joint research efforts drive innovation, increase competitiveness and technological progress.

Investing in research creates a knowledge-based economy that promotes long-term growth and prosperity. Ensuring collective security promotes stability across Europe and creates a secure environment for the economic activites and investments. A well-regulated financial sector boosts investor confidence and facilitates the cross-border movement of capital. Sound financial systems must ensure economic stability and resilience to external shocks. They promote diplomatic efforts and reduce geopolitical risks that could affect economic stability.

A unified foreign policy makes it possible to strengthen Europe's influence on the world stage and enables strategic partnerships and trade agreements. Efficient infrastructure and connectivity facilitate trade, commerce and the movement of goods and services. The use of digital connectivity increases productivity and competitiveness in the digital economy.

A collapse disproportionately affects usually the most vulnerable populations, exacerbating social inequality and leading to increased poverty. Essential public services, such as healthcare and education, could become disrupted, severely impacting the quality of life and future opportunities for citizens.This distrust can lead to social unrest and a lack of faith in political leaders. Future-oriented systems are increasingly designed with sustainability in mind. Their collapse can halt environmental progress and worsen climate change impacts. Effective resource management systems, which are crucial for a sustainable development, are being undermined, leading to waste and depletion of natural resources.

Nationalist parties tend to pursue toxic policies characterized by hostility, division and irrationality that hinder progress and cooperation. „Party-apparatus democracy" is a form of democracy in which the closed party apparatus takes precedence over individual opinions. This form of democracy is characterized by abuse of power and authoritarian structures, which makes it difficult to find a rational solution in parliaments. It is no longer important which party says what or not, it is much more about what is important for the addressees. The specific needs of voters are becoming the focus.

How can governments function, if multiple groups debate decision-making? Because in the future it will be difficult to achieve absolute or even effective relative majorities. In the absence of a one-party majority, multiple factions can work together to reach decisions in government. These decisions are typically based on negotiated agreements that establish common policy objectives and governance principles. This involves seeking broad agreement across the different groups on key issues, rather than relying solely on simple majority votes. Consensus politics can help avoid extreme polarization and foster stability. In situations where consensus is difficult to achieve, decentralization of power to regional or local governments can help. This allows different regions to implement policies that reflect their unique needs and preferences while maintaining overall unity.

Rather than forming a full coalition, political groups may form issue-based alliances, where they agree to cooperate on specific policies while maintaining independence on other matters. This allows for flexibility in governance and can lead to innovative solutions. Independent institutions, such as constitutional courts, electoral commissions and ombudsman offices can play a central role in maintaining the rule of law and ensuring that the government functions smoothly, even in a fragmented political environment. In deeply divided parliaments, professional mediators or facilitators can be brought in to help manage negotiations between the groups, ensuring that dialogue remains constructive and that agreements are reached.

Ideological debates fade into the background, while the immediate concerns and challenges are addressed. The individual credibility and trust in the personality of politicians are becoming more important than the party program to which they belong. Practical political discussions are increasingly focusing on specific issues rather than relying on broad ideological concepts. Instead of parties, new formats will take over the role and fight for the voters' favor.

Society plays a distinctive role in shaping political developments and promoting cooperation. Overcoming nationalistic tendencies, showing openness for cooperation, it is easier to work towards a more prosperous and sustainable world for all. Paradigm shifts can have unexpected consequences that are difficult to predict. These consequences can be positive or negative and require thorough analysis and monitoring. A paradigm shift usually means that political decisions and strategies are reconsidered and changed. This can lead to uncertainty about how governments will act in the future. When political decisions and measures are changed, economic conditions and the business environment will also change. This in turn has an impact on companies, investors, jobs and society as a whole.

It is extremely worrying when wealthy magnates like in the USA, in connection with dictatorial-infected politicians, influence politics and put their own interests before the welfare of society. In such cases, it is crucial to raise awareness and encourage actors and civil society to take action against this form of economic and political despotism. Through targeted public relations and international cooperation, competitors could inform the public about the negative effects of such activities. The role of the civil society should not be underestimated in taking action through their consumer behavior against companies that engage in vicious practices. By engaging in conscious consumption and supporting ethical businesses, consumers are called to contribute sending a message against the power and influence of despots in business and politics.

When policymakers focus solely on short-term gains or narrow national interests, they may overlook the broader impacts of their decisions on a global scale. This can lead to missed opportunities for collective actions and shared solutions, that could benefit all countries and communities. Furthermore, the lack of cooperation and solidarity in global politics can exacerbate existing inequalities and injustices, as resources and opportunities may not be distributed fairly. Without a common approach to addressing challenges, vulnerable populations are often left behind, deepening poverty, exacerbating environmental degradation and perpetuating conflict. If the decisions are not taken correctly at the content level, this is also to the detriment of all countries in all geographical areas.

The relevance of focusing on social welfare lies in a more sustainable and inclusive political design. When policy decisions aim to improve the well-being of the entire population, measures will be taken that promote long-term social stability and prosperity, rather than maximize short-term economic gains. This is particularly important in a globalised world where social inequalities and environmental problems are transnational.

The struggle for co-creation in international politics refers to various aspects of collaboration and interaction between citizens, scientists and policymakers. This can help to prevent resistance to change, increase the likelihood of successful implementation and ultimately improve the overall quality of governance. The most important strategies for effective stakeholder management in politics include regular contacts with stakeholders through various communication channels, such as public consultations and open round-table discussions. It also involves relationships based on trust and mutual respect, as well as being open and transparent about decision-making processes.

Structural solutions emerge through a systematic process of evaluation, analysis, and decision-making. Initially, the respective current state is carefully evaluated and analyzed. This involves identifying relevant factors, that impact the existing system. A thorough analysis forms the foundation for understanding the current structures, their weaknesses and their strengths. Based on this analysis, various solution options are subsequently developed. Each option is gauged in terms of feasibility, efficiency and potential impact. This weighing process is crucial to understanding the advantages and disadvantages of the different alternatives for making an informed decision. It is important to consider both short-term and long-term perspectives to develop sustainable solutions.

In order to effectively evaluate the current state of a system using empirical formulas, a structured approach is required. The aim is to determine key parameters that influence the system. This may include statistical models, linear programming or other techniques. Key metrics provide insight into data trends and variability. Tools like regression analysis and control charts help uncover underlying problems and their causes. This often involves comparing current performance with benchmarks or standards. They are the basis for recommendations to improving systems, optimizing processes, redesigning work processes or other implementations. All considerations on the way to the decision are there to create the conviction that society is able to live self-determined and freely.

Only after a thorough analysis of the different options, priorities emerge, that lead to a decision for the most appropriate solution. This means that decisions are not based on assumptions or insufficient data but on solid analysis and clear evidence. Through this methodical approach, it can be ensured that the chosen solution is not only effective but also efficient and sustainable. This ultimately leads to improved outcomes and a more stable, high-performing system.

One of the biggest problems in the current shaping of European politics is the power dynamics between the different actors. Traditional hierarchies often hinder effective collaboration, as decision-making is often concentrated in the hands of a few individuals. This can lead to a lack of diverse perspectives and innovative solutions being considered in policy-making processes. The complexity of global issues such as climate change, migration and conflict require a multidisciplinary approach that includes input from various stakeholders. However, differences in values, interests, and priorities among different actors can create tensions and hinder effective co-creation.

To overcome these difficulties it is essential to prioritize inclusivity, diversity and transparency in decision-making processes. This can be achieved through mechanisms such as participatory democracy, citizen assemblies, and the inclusion of diverse voices in policy-making forums. Transparency, accountability, and open communication are essential for building consensus and ensuring that co-created policies are grounded in the needs and priorities of all stakeholders.

Consulting agencies are the ones that deal with presentation and political communication. However, if they become too one-sided in their techniques, their capacity for problem solving decreases. A paradigm shift in politics should always lead to positive changes and opportunities for progress. For example, a shift towards more sustainable and environmentally friendly policies can lead to the growth of green industries and new job opportunities in renewable energy, conservation and sustainable agriculture. This is not only to the advantage of the environment but also creates economic growth and improves living standards. In order to achieve general progress, several factors are important: future orientation means a clear vision and the willingness to pursue risky strategies.

Semantic strategy is a guiding principle that rewards the future for what happens in the present, regardless of specific events. Progress as a collective singularity means the universalization of progress in various fields, such as science, art, law, morality, politics and economics, all of which strive for a similar goal. Knowledge and application are necessary to solve problems and make progress. It is not good for the belief in political progress, if people do not understand the facts or do not want to understand them.

It is important for governments, companies and individuals to adapt to the paradigm shifts and actively shape the future. Th success is additionally forged by a perfect communication in implementing new policies and regulations, investing in new technologies and changing behaviors and practices. Collaboration and cooperation between different stakeholders are the key to navigating these changes successfully and maximizing the positive outcomes. In particular, greater consideration should be given to the complex network structures and other factors that influence the design of decision-making. The aim is to examine how political management affects the development and what factors influence its effectiveness.

Both, top-down and bottom-up approaches in policy implementation are necessary to capture the complexities of engagement at global, national and local levels. Higher-level goals and strategies are specified top-down in order to coordinate their implementation. Decisions are made at an overview and then implemented at broader levels. At the same time, the needs and realities are integrated bottom-up at the base and thus adapted to local circumstances.

Paradigm shifts bring new perspectives and uncertainties and offer opportunities for positive change and progress. By predicting possible consequences and observing developments, the future is not defenceless. The work must be done to respect international norms and human rights and oppose all forms of aggression, discrimination and oppression. Pragmatic approaches in international politics emphasize the need to find realistic and practical solutions. They take into account the actual circumstances and interests of smaller or larger entities in order to develop effective strategies. Constructivism, on the other hand, means that social structures and institutions in international relations are artificially constructed. Essential principles of international law are based on rules, that are repeatedly relativized, changed or disregarded in the practice. Pragmatic approaches emphasize the need to find realistic solutions that take account of actual interests and circumstances.

Through dialogue, alliances can effectively address global challenges and conflicts rather than resort to confrontational and power-driven methods. Reforming international institutions and partnerships can improve cooperation and strengthen collective responses to common threats. A too one-sided focus on diplomacy does not lead to positive results. In dealing with countries or actors that pose a threat to global security and stability, it is important to strike a balance between peaceful negotiations and determination, sometimes backed by sanctions. If only single countries impose sanctions, the sanctioned country can find ways to circumvent them by doing business with non-sanctioning countries. Global coordination minimizes such loopholes.

A coordinated international response requires a strong,

united front against misconduct by diverse dictatorships. If sanctions are circumvented, secondary sanctions promise additional success. This penalizes third parties who continue to do business with sanctioned countries. For instance in the Ukraine conflict, the continued exploitation of loopholes is having a serious impact, leading to the loss of countless lives and the continuation of violence. Not a day since the attack on Ukraine, ordered by Putin, goes without bombs on the civilian population and without violent deaths. Who supports these conditions? The blame lies with companies interested in their own profits and with provocative supporters on the extremist flanks of the inner-European spectrum. Sanctions violators or extremist politicians who support dictators in their war attacks should, like the criminal dictators themselves, be held accountable. Stronger international action, improved enforcement and enhanced cooperation should curb aggression and increase the prospects for a peaceful solution.

History offers numerous examples of the convincing effects of sanctions: the dismantling of the Iron Curtain in 1989, which occurred due to military and economic pressure on the Soviet Union as an indirect form of sanction politics; Spain's transition to democracy after the death of dictator Franco or the end of apartheid policies in South Africa, all demonstrate how sanctions can lead to significant political changes.

The idea that absolute security can be achieved is an illusion. In reality, there is always some degree of uncertainty and risk. There are always unforeseeable events that cannot be fully controlled or prevented. However, this does not mean that caution and prevention should be neglected. Despite the impossibility of eliminating all risks, it is essential to take preventive measures and prepare for possible crisis situations. This can be achieved through various security measures. An alert and well-prepared community can better respond to threats and minimize their impact. Because threats and risks are constantly evolving, security measures must also be continually reviewed and adjusted. This requires flexibility and the willingness to learn from experience and adapt to new challenges.

Preventive diplomacy in the early stages of a conflict are crucial to prevent escalation, provided it is conducted preemptively and harshly. But there is often a lack of political will and resources to implement such preventative measures. Governments tend to respond only after violence has already escalated, making the situation even worse. Another problem is the insufficient coordination between different leaders, which makes prevention measures ineffective.

The consequences of delayed conflict prevention are catastrophic: massive outbreaks of violence, armed conflicts, humanitarian crises, refugee flows, regional destabilization and long-term traumatization of entire societies. The costs of peacekeeping and reconstruction far exceed the investments in prevention. In order to avoid such disasters, early warning systems and conflict analyzes must be optimized. Human rights violations must be punished consistently from the outset. Only through early and decisive action by the international community escalation of violence and humanitarian disasters can be prevented. Prevention must therefore be the top priority in international politics. Unfortunately, governments tend to only respond after violence has already escalated, which often makes the situation worse.

Newly emerging economies should ideally focus on promoting education, skills development and entrepreneurship among their populations in order to fully exploit their economic potential. By investing in human capital and creating opportunities for all individuals to participate in the economy, countries can reduce poverty and inequality and ultimately achieve sustainable economic growth. It is important that all stakeholders - governments, international organizations and companies - work together to tackle the causes of poverty and promote economic development. By implementing comprehensive and inclusive strategies, a more prosperous and fairer development for all can be projected.

New busines models offer advantages such as the simplification of regulatory structures and the improvement of operational efficiency. If crises have already reached the immediate environment, it is necessary to prepare for the impending changes, be it financially or economically or to restrict lifestyle habits. This applies in particular to wealthy and pampered structures. Everything can be trained. By proactively adjusting to challenges, building resilience, and supporting one another, individuals and communities can navigate crises effectively and emerge stronger, more resilient and better prepared for future challenges. Adaptation and resilience are essential for overcoming uncertainties and building a more sustainable and prosperous future.

A nationalistic economic policy, which often goes hand in hand with protectionist measures ignores the realities of a globalized economy. In an interconnected world, economies are increasingly interdependent. The idea that a nation can successfully manage its economy through purely nationalistic reasoning and local practices, is a dangerous illusion. The global economy today is so interdependent that nationalism and isolationism inevitably lead to significant economic damage. Numerous historical and current events in world politics and economics prove that countries that rely on nationalistic strategies always fail. A nationalistic economic policy hinders in the end a country's ability to innovate. Global supply chains, international financial markets and technological progress make it almost impossible to view or control economic developments in isolation. Subsidies for uncompetitive industries often only delay the necessary structural change. In addition, currency manipulation has unintended negative consequences for domestic economies.

However, the relationship between a European industrial policy and strict competition supervision also reveals tensions. Both pursue different, but not necessarily contradictory objectives. While industrial policy aims to promote strategic sectors and strengthen economic competitiveness, competition supervision focuses on ensuring fair market conditions and preventing monopolies. The EU Commission is committed to ensuring that all member states adhere to the same competition rules in order to guarantee uniform market conditions.

Nevertheless, a national protectionist industrial policy could destabilize the internal market. In the face of intense international competition and rapid technological developments, European industrial policy aims to strengthen key industries, drive technological innovation and promote sustainable economic growth. This strategy is crucial to positioning Europe as a global innovation leader and securing the EU's economic future. By investing in clean energy technologies and expanding its energy infrastructure, Europe aims to play a leading role in the global fight against climate change. At the same time, the competitiveness of European industry will be strengthened through a stable and sustainable energy supply.

Infrastructure is another area in which the EU is focusing its industrial policy. The expansion of modern transport and communication networks is essential to strengthening the single market, facilitating cross-border trade and driving forward the digital transformation. An equally important cornerstone of European industrial policy is the promotion of research and development. Programs such as "Horizon Europe" support research institutions, universities and companies to develop ground-breaking technologies and gain new scientific knowledge. The promotion of R&D is additionally an important factor in the creation of high-quality jobs.. These jobs not only contribute to economic stability, but also promote social and economic inclusion by creating well-paid employment opportunities across Europe.

This targeted funding also includes measures aimed at supporting small and medium-sized companies, which form the real backbone of the European economy. By creating favorable framework conditions and providing access to financing, SMEs should be enabled to grow and remain innovative. By promoting "green technologies" and supporting initiatives to decarbonize industry, the EU is helping to reduce environmental impact while ensuring long-term competitiveness. This is important not only from an environmental perspective, but also to successfully manage the transition to a climate-neutral economy.

Another key concern of the EU is the fight against tax avoidance and tax evasion. In recent years, several directives have been adopted to prevent aggressive tax planning and unfair tax practices. In many cases, tax policy decisions at EU level require the unanimous agreement of the member states. This makes it difficult to push through far-reaching reforms or greater harmonization, as each country can use a veto, if it feels its national interests are at risk. This is one more reason to restructure the European Council.

Although Europe as a whole faces challenges such as bureaucracy, skills shortages and energy insecurity, it can offer significantly more benefits and attractiveness to businesses and investors as a common economic area than individual countries could. The size of the market, the infrastructure and economic integration make Europe as a whole a special attractive business location.

Nevertheless, it is important to bear in mind that Europe is facing considerable demographic challenges, including an ageing population and falling birth rates in many member states. This is leading to a shrinking working population, which is hampering the economic growth. An aging population also means higher expenditure on healthcare and pension systems, which increases the fiscal burden on states and could limit investment in other growth areas.

Moreover, it is not encouraging that in recent years the EU has fallen behind the US and China in some key technological areas, particularly in areas such as artificial intelligence, digital platforms and 5G technologies. These countries have made significant progress, while the EU has struggled to keep up with the pace of innovation. The energy crisis in the wake of the Ukraine war has exposed the EU's weaknesses in this area and could slow the economic growth, if effective alternatives are not found.

The EU's economic importance may decline relatively for a variety of reasons, due to internal challenges such as demographic changes and political disunity, and external factors such as the rise of new economic powers and global technological developments. In order to counteract this trend, measures such as reducing bureaucracy, promoting innovation, improving energy supply and a stronger common foreign and economic policy are considered necessary. Although the EU remains one of the largest economies in the world, it needs to actively address these challenges in order to maintain and strengthen its economic relevance in the global context.

The economic advantage of establishing „macro-regions"
is obvious, because they have detailed insight into their
widely intertwined economic structures, including the
peculiarities of the industrial and service sectors. These
constructions would allow them to tailor to the specific
needs of their geographies. So they receive a direct
feedback from companies and other local interest
groups. While the center in Brussels has oversight of
macroeconomic developments, internal market rules,
international trade policies and overarching economic
policies aimed at long-term integration and stability,
individual regions have more detailed knowledge of the
local economies and the proximity to address the needs
of their citizens directly. An optimal economic overview
is secured through the coordination of both levels.
The European economy will certainly not kept running by
extremist political fringe groups or rigid, outdated
political traditions. Their views threaten economic

stability and growth by undermining key market mechanisms, discouraging investment and hindering international trade. The economic incompetence of the extremist positions lies in their inability to provide sustainable and viable solutions to the challenges of globalization, technological changes and demographic change. At the same time, long-established political habits also pose risks for Europe's economic dynamism. While traditional parties tend to cling to outdated practices, they prevent necessary reforms from being implemented in areas of digitalization, energy policy or the labor market. Europe's economic situation is better determined by a pragmatic approach that emphasizes both economic expertise and innovative solutions.

You see "own goals" in soccer, but also in politics, where they are even more unpleasant. They cause long-term disasters that affect not only those responsible, but the entire country and community. They damage trust in government, undermine public confidence and hinder progress. In extreme cases, own goals disguised as self-interest in politics can lead to crises, conflicts and even the destabilization of a country. The consequences are economic downturn, social unrest and a deterioration in international relations. It can take years or even decades to recover from the repercussions of political own goals. Therefore, political decision-makers have always to act responsibly, make well-informed decisions and prioritize the interests of the public over short-term political gains. By avoiding their own missteps, they help ensure the prosperity, stability and well-being of their countries and communities. When we watch them stumble through international crises like little children through a china shop and leave behind a trail of broken alliances and economic disasters, do we feel good? Who needs Netflix when real politics offers so much drama and unintentional comedy?

In the first two decades of the 21st century, politics in some european countries was often misled by unqualified political leaders. On the one hand, the inability of some German top politicians to be politically innovative, has even caused domestic political difficulties for its long-time partner France, while on the other hand, the misjudgment of the Kremlin policy has led to the important Eastern European region being neglected. This has weakened important partnerships and created the impression of having lost touch with current developments.

It would have to be clear that in the complex web of European politics, the relationships between member states form the basis for cooperation, unity and progress. However, recent developments have highlighted a worrying trend in Germany's attitude towards its European partners, particularly France, which raises questions about the country's commitment within the

European Union. Germany should rethink its approach and return to shared visions and strategies in order to actively work towards building a stronger, united Europe.

Germany, once seen as an important partner in shaping common policy for the EU, appears to be moving away from that central role, creating a dangerous divide at the core of European power dynamics. Instead of actively engaging in constructive cooperation, chancellor Scholz's approach is characterized by the fact that he prefers to distance himself from those who are committed to change and innovation, following in the footsteps of his predecessor chancellor Angela Merkel. This changing attitude towards European politics is exacerbated by the weak rhetorical communication, which affects the ability to influence decision-making and shape the future of the EU. The traditional axis between Germany and France, often cited as the driving force behind the European project, is showing signs of tension and weakening the European construct.

How are you supposed to get along with France if you don't understand your neighbor culturally well enough? The same phenomenon applies even more to the relationship with the eastern partner Poland. It was the shortcoming of a German chancellorship that, due to its exaggerated self-image, it did not understand the common Europe at all, because it was not wanted at all. Maybe it was wrong political socialization. It starts with learning your neighbor's language. It is an important requirement for international communication. Now the young generation is starting to rethink their exchange functions. While Germany is often known for its efficiency and punctuality, French culture places great value on sociability, enjoyment and direct communication. These differences can lead to misunderstandings that are noticeable in both personal and professional contexts.

Germans moving to France often have to learn that the French way of life requires a different approach to time and social interactions. A similar phenomenon of misunderstanding can be seen in the relationship with Poland. Historical prejudices and stereotypical ideas play a role that make mutual understanding difficult. A lack of language skills and cultural misjudgments often lead to some people not sufficiently appreciating or understanding the nature of others, which hinders collaboration.

At a time when strong leadership and unity are crucial to addressing the challenges facing Europe, a departure from the common goals and principles of the European project poses a significant risk to the cohesion and effectiveness of the Union. As one of the EU's most influential member states Germany plays a central role in shaping the future of European politics. It is urgent that Germany's politicians rethink their approach and refocus on shared visions and strategies. The best thing to do is to work actively with the other Europeans to build a stronger, more united Europe and not just wait and see what happens. Moreover, the weakeness in the aspirations of the „Weimar Triangle" has weakened important intra-European relations and undermined progress in the European integration. The Weimar Triangle, consisting of France, Germany and Poland, has begun ist activities in 1991. However, the format has been largely dormant for the past decade due to differing visions among the members on the EU-future. It led to a loss of momentum in addressing key issues such as security, migration and economic cooperation. This trend was driven by Germany's strategic interests in securing access to Russia's vast natural resources and lucrative markets. As a result, Germany became heavily reliant on Russian energy imports, particularly natural gas, which made it vulnerable to potential disruptions in supply.

These factors have contributed to threats to democratic values, the rule of law and human rights in some other countries. In addition, the ignorance of citizens' needs and concerns led to a growing loss of trust in politics. The lack of willingness to pursue an active and responsible foreign policy has caused Europe to partially fall behind. Instead of actively participating in international conflicts and taking a leadership role, some governments have retreated into comfortable passivity. This means that influence on the international stage was lost.

When critics then intervene with arguments that foreign policy leaders should act diplomatically, this is a recipe for stirring up ignorance and uncertainty. It should be known that although foreign ministers head diplomatic authorities, their job description is that of active helmsmen. While other countries developed innovative solutions, Europe's economically strongest country remained stuck in old ways of thinking. As a result, it has lost touch with important issues of the future.

Why is impulsive-creative leadership so rare in German politics? The fact that German political leadership is often perceived as boring or humorless compared to its neighbors is due to cultural differences and the strange socialist heritage, which maneuvers in the background and shapes the political landscape. It is known for its emphasis on stability and thoroughness in governance, which can sometimes be perceived as a lack of spontaneity, charm and a more relaxed political style common in other countries. Deficits in the political class can pose a threat to global political prosperity. It will not be easy to escape this trap as political competitiveness becomes weaker.

The role of foreign ministers in shaping diplomatic policy and representing their countries' positions in international forums is of central importance.

Interference by a chancellery can undermine the effectiveness of diplomatic efforts and thus jeopardize the credibility of the country's international engagement. The diplomatic efforts are closely linked to the credibility of its leadership. If foreign ministers are not allowed to act independently, this can undermine trust with other nations and lead to instability and disorder in international relations.

The need for effective global governance is becoming increasingly urgent, particularly when addressing serious problems like climate change, terrorism and the governance of emerging technologies. However, the lack of autonomy and independence in diplomatic decision-making can hinder the ability to address these challenges effectively. The current political environment is characterized by a global credibility gap, in which the lack of serious commitments and the erosion of trust have led to remarkable governance deficits. These are exacerbated when diplomatic efforts are influenced by state self-interest rather than a genuine commitment to global cooperation and the common good.

Efforts could be made to reform global governance structures in order to better meet the challenges of the modern world. This includes the development of global guidelines that provide a framework for international cooperation and the harmonization of goals. Decision-making processes should be more inclusive and involve not only state actors but also civil society groups. This would take into account the interests of many stakeholders and make global governance more representative and effective.

The European Union is proving to be a unique phenomenon on the road to the future. It has the potential to be a role model also to outside its own area. However, it will only be able to function for all other tasks, once it has created the basis for security. The well-being of future generations on this continent depends on the will for unity and the strength of its political union. Without growth, there are no social models and no other added value. Growth comes best from unity. Establishing it requires diligence, perseverance and assertiveness.

It is convenient to sleep on politics for too long, but the leadership will inevitably be backed into a corner because ignoring or neglecting political issues for too long will have negative consequences. This means that avoiding or evading policy challenges or responsibilities will ltimately catch up with leaders and hold them accountable or will result in consequences. Dynamism and efficiency of action require flexibility, otherwise everything will shatter into a thousand pieces. It is therefore important for political leaders to stay informed, respond to the needs and concerns of constituents and navigate the complex political landscape.

In a rapidly changing and interconnected world, political leaders must be able to deal with uncertainty, complexity and competing interests in an agile and forward-looking manner. This is especially true in a crisis environment of military conflict. Rapid and effective action must then be taken, in collaboration with a trusted advisory team. There are a variety of ways to do this, including military interventions, economic embargoes or humanitarian interventions. Their legitimacy and morality are often the subject of fierce debate, as they raise complex ethical questions. Ultimately, the debate on interventionism reflects the tension between different moral principles and political interests. International politics is not a lottery.

Deterrence is absolutely essential for maintaining peace. A strong military presence and the ability to retaliate quickly and effectively will deter a potential aggressor, because the costs and risks of attack are too high. If all parties know that an attack would lead to devastating retaliation, the likelihood of a rash or irrational attack is reduced. This promotes a stable international order. In addition, deterrence helps to prevent smaller conflicts from escalating into larger wars, as all sides are aware of the possible consequences.

It is important that European leaders recognize the importance of skilled decision-making in shaping the continent's future. They just need to prioritize political competence in leadership positions and actively work to create innovative and inclusive policies that meet the needs and concerns of all European citizens. This includes strengthening relations beyond the Eastern European regions. Once Putin's unspeakable aggression is over, there will have to be a dialogue with Russia. The principles of democracy, human rights and the rule of law must be respected. Only the eastern wing of Europe can extend a hand of peace to Russia. Therefore, the main task will be to politically and economically strengthen the Eastern European area, which has been a defining part of European culture for centuries.

By prioritizing political competency, European leaders can work towards restoring trust in politics, strengthening important partnerships and safeguarding democratic values across the continent. Only through proactive and informed decision-making Europe will positively navigate through the complexity of the 21st century and emerge as a united and resilient force on the global stage.

On the other side of the Atlantic, an unleashed „wild-west-hero" has thrown the world into turmoil as he shot down longstanding international agreements and institutions in favor of a more isolationist and unilateral approach. This has created uncertainty and instability on the global stage, as traditional allies question the reliability of the United States as a partner. In Russia his counterpart, an unscrupulous dictator, has consolidated power and cracked down on dissent, leading to increased tensions with Western countries. Russia's interference in foreign elections, the annexation of Crimea and the brutal attack on Ukraine, as well as the cruel involvement in the conflict in Syria, have severely strained the relations with the international community.

Dictators begin their rule on thin ice and must be ruthless in consolidating their power. They often use deception and manipulation to control their people and eliminate resistance. Over time, they become more and more self-confident and use any means to maintain their power. The more power dictators gain, the more brazen they become, leading to unpredictable and destructive behavior that harms more than just the people. Their rule is therefore characterized by violence, oppression and fear, leaving behind a legacy of suffering and destruction. Fascist laws are applied quickly. This shows people's willingness to commit political suicide. At the same time, on the other side of society, the capacity for compassion, empathy and resistance to injustice is a fundamental part of the human experience and essential to encourage those who fight against tyranny and fascism in all its forms.

Dictatorships use various expansive forces to extend their power and control over their territory and beyond. These expansionary forces can be related to different areas, including political, economic, social, and military aspects. Usually dictatorships solidify their power by suppressing political opposition, restricting freedom of speech and manipulating elections. They even try to extend their political agenda to other countries, by influencing international organizations or by supporting authoritarian regimes in other countries to expand their regional or global power. Economically, dictatorships advance their expansion through economic exploitation, corruption, and creating dependencies in other countries. They try to influence the economy of other countries through investments and trade relationships. Socially, modern dictatorships use their expansionary forces through propaganda, suppression of minorities, and control of the media to spread their ideology and control the population. Militarily, dictatorships advance their expansion through the use of force, intervention in other countries, and the modernization of their armed forces to protect their own territorial integrity and advance their regional or global interests.

Authoritarian regimes in Asia give cause for concern about the human rights situation in their region. Countries such as China and North Korea have been accused of widespread human rights abuses, including political repression, censorship and the suppression of dissent. The political environment has been characterized by uncertainty, instability and a lack of reasonable leadership. There is a risk, that the foundations of international peace and security will be further undermined.

Some rulers may simply be motivated by a desire for power, leading it to manipulate democratic systems for personal gain. This can manifest in various forms, such as manipulating elections, curtailing press freedom, or engaging in corruption and nepotism. The erosion of democratic norms in some countries has further exacerbated the situation, leading to a weakening of the separation of powers and an increase in corruption and abuse of power. Lack of respect for human rights and the rule of law has contributed further deepening the cycle of instability and injustice. With the return to democratic structures, the attempts to destroy social values could be abolished. In any case, it is important for democratic societies to remain vigilant and guard against attempts to undermine their principles and institutions. This will be achieved through strong control mechanisms, transparency, accountability and an alert and engaged civil society.

The development of authoritarian tendencies in Hungary and Poland is a serious concern, as these governments have taken steps to undermine democratic institutions and consolidate political control. In Poland, the PiS party has used its electoral mandate to carry out judicial reforms tied to political authoritarianism, which have been criticized by the Venice Commission as undermining the rule of law. A dominant party passed a law giving the justice minister the power to appoint and dismiss court presidents. How can a society fall for the manipulation of manipulative governments? Similarly, in Hungary, the Fidesz party under Prime Minister Viktor Orbán recorded a decline in the country's performance on key governance indicators, coupled with a decline in standards of the rule of law and accountability. The party has also sought to exert control overthe state-funded media. These actions by the governments in Hungary and Poland indicate a concerning trend toward authoritarianism, as they seek to consolidate power and weaken democratic checks and balances. What a snubbing danger, if others wanted to imitate this!

Politicians may exploit fear, anger or other strong emotions to sway public opinion and garner support for their policies. This involves exaggerating threats or creating scapegoats. Fanaticism is not only nourished from the air. It includes a mixture of terror, sadism and violence. It is the task of the European Union and the international community to closely monitor such developments and take measures to protect democratic principles and the rule of law. Incompetent and selfish people in power tend to overestimate their own abilities and underestimate the competencies of others. This is because they are unable to recognize the extent of their incompetence. The exaggerated ruler mentality leads to an exaggerated perception of one's own abilities. They may believe that their judgments and decisions are inherently better than those of others, leading to unhealthy optimism and preventing them from seeking input or admitting mistakes.

Aggressive states that only understand the language of violence believe they can benefit from overestimating their power. This approach should be countered with determination and wisdom. If the co-creation of the peoples of Europe in the spirit of the musketeer ethos of "one for all, all for one" does not begin in time, there will be no attractive strategies for the future. The fateful questions between freedom and violence depend on this.

Conflicts in Syria, Yemen, Iraq orPalastine have led to widespread humanitarian crises and instability in the region. The former rise of terrorist groups such as ISIS has posed a threat to global security, leading to military interventions by various countries. In Africa, political instability, corruption, and poverty continue to hinder development and progress in many countries. Conflicts in countries such as South Sudan, Somalia, and the Democratic Republic of Congo have resulted in widespread displacement and humanitarian crises. Tackling these global problems requires a coordinated approach by the international community. Cooperation between countries, multilateral institutions and non-governmental organizations is essential for the promotion of peace, security and development on a global scale.

A fundamental task of international politics is to prioritize diplomacy, dialogue and cooperation. What happens in one part of the world can have immediately far-reaching impacts that affect people and ecosystems all around the world. For example, the burning of fossil fuels in one country contributes to global climate change, which affects weather patterns and sea levels in other parts of the world. Pollution in one region can spread through air and water currents, affecting ecosystems and human health in distant places. Globalization has connected economies, making them vulnerable to economic crises in one country that can spread immediately to other countries.

Due to the interconnectedness of the global economy, events such as natural disasters or political conflicts in one country have a global impact on supply chains, trade relationships and financial markets. They affect companies, employees and consumers in numerous countries. The international community therefore has the task of working together to isolate authoritarian regimes and stop their machinations. This includes measures such as economic sanctions, diplomatic pressure, targeted military actions and support for democratic movements in affected countries. In some continents, the root causes of structural decay lie in poverty, injustice, political oppression and lack of education opportunities. Long-term development programs could help reduce the influence and power of anarchic systems.

If the intended structural change is not addressed somewhat internationally, the results would be suboptimal at best. Most economic, technological, environmental and social challenges therefore require global coordination. The effects of climate change can only be brought under control if countries around the world work together. Emissions reductions and the transition to clean energy require coordinated action around the world. Building a sustainable future on this planet requires global approaches, because technological developments do not stop at national borders. In order to remain competitive, countries must be able to exchange ideas and strengthen their innovation capacities.

Drawing parallels means broadening perspectives, questioning assumptions and promoting critical thinking. By recognizing patterns and similarities between different topics or situations, deeper meanings and hidden connections become apparent. This is the only way to make informed decisions and to deal with complex problems more effectively. These processes require openness and a willingness to explore different viewpoints. It's about looking beyond superficial differences and looking at the underlying similarities that aren't immediately apparent.

B. HOPE FOR GLOBAL-ORIENTED POLITICS

Hope is an essential aspect of political considerations, particularly in the context of overlapping crises such as concurrent climate change, economic inequality and threats to democracy. Hope is an essential part of global politics because it inspires action and experimentation for a better future. Political hope must be distinguished from fear. The responsibility and the pursuit of a more democratic society must be recognized at an early stage.

Historically, fear-based politics have always encouraged nationalist thinking. Fear is a powerful tool for political reactionaries, while hope inspires rational political action. Narratives of hope shape the structure and direction of positive politics. These requirements cannot be effectively addressed by any single country alone. As awareness of these issues grows, there is increasing pressure on policymakers to prioritize international cooperation and find solutions that benefit more and more countries.

The Global South and Global North can indeed be pitted against each other, particularly in areas such as trade, finance and geopolitics. In trade, many argue that the North exploits the South by sourcing cheap raw materials and labor and exporting expensive products. The South is trying to take collective countermeasures in order to achieve fairer trade relations. Major powers such as China, Russia and India are expanding their presence in the global south to gain economic and political influence. They provide financial support, infrastructure and trade opportunities to developing countries to pursue their own interests and limit Western influence. When it comes to climate policy, some countries in the South argue that the North has historically contributed more to climate change and should therefore bear more responsibility.

They demand financial aid and technology transfer, which leads to tensions.

However, there are also many common interests between North and South, such as fighting poverty, terrorism or pandemics. Many countries are working together on these issues. Nevertheless, it is important to be aware of the dynamics of playing off one another and to look for ways in which the Global South can better represent its interests and help shape a fairer global order. When it comes to global partnerships, collaboration for mutual benefit must be prioritized. This happens when partnerships are equal and sustainable. With a view to protecting the multipolar order, the diversity of perspectives and interests in the global community must be respected.

In communication, the dialogue with global partners has to be transparent and open. The exchange of information promotes the search for common ground with common goals. There are also cases in which it could be necessary to forego certain privileges or advantages in order to consolidate greater cooperation and solidarity in the global community. This may mean making sacrifices for the greater good.

International politics must continually address the existential questions of systems that are intended to continually develop security aspects. It is therefore necessary that the international community has mechanisms in place to regularly review existing security guarantees and adapt them to the circumstances. This includes various tools that focus on addressing global problems. Classical theories emphasize the role of the state as key actor in international politics. They regard states as homogeneous units with specific interests. However, this perspective is seen as too narrow and no longer appropriate for the realities of the 21st century.

Liberal theories assume that people, as rational decision-makers, can create the long-term conditions for the successful pursuit of interests in changed structures. They presuppose that people are prepared to relate their own claim to freedom to the claim to freedom of all other people. However, these approaches are often criticized for not sufficiently taking into account the structural conditions, that limit the ability of individuals and groups to act. Institutional approaches focus on the role of institutions and collaboration working together to solve global problems. They emphasize the importance of transnational cooperation and the ability of international and regional institutions to take on tasks, that states alone can no longer manage. Structuralist approaches assume that the relationships within a system determine the actors' ability to act. They emphasize the role of power and conflicts of interest in shaping international politics.

It has always been the case that there have always been negative elements in world politics. Nevertheless there was again and again the strength to fight back. This requires persistence and commitment to global cooperation, especially today. International relations are often characterized by negative power, uncertainty and conflicts of interest, even if this does not always correspond to normative ideals. What you don't want to believe is often a bitter reality. Realistic theories assume, that states primarily strive to maintain and expand power, even if this may be morally questionable. Human rights and democracy are often sacrificed for „realpolitik". Without mandated authority, states find themselves in a constant struggle for security and influence. Cooperation is difficult and conflict is common. Despite the proliferation of international law and institutions, the disorder in international relations has often increased. States, not nations, remain the most powerful actors. Given the complexity of world politics, no theory can predict or explain all phenomena.

In a world where communication increasingly takes place via social media and digital platforms, the value of face-to-face communication should not be lost sight of. Direct, face-to-face communication provides greater clarity and understanding in conversations and helps build stronger connections. Staying informed, always seeking new experiences and evaluating direct communication accordingly means a more hopeful future for everyone. It is everyone's right to learn about policies instead of relying solely on biased sources or social media. Critically analyzing different perspectives and searching for credible sources ensures an informed opinion. It is the first step towards a meaningful political discussion.

Additionally, it is every individual's right to educate themselves about policies rather than relying solely on biased sources. The public has a right to transparency in international politics. Even if evaluation is often suppressed in the environment of large organizations, the feedback from civil society brings its demands to the surface. Evaluation can no longer be abolished or suppressed. Critically analyzing different perspectives and searching for credible sources ensures an informed opinion. This is a big step towards a meaningful political discussion.

The fact base always refers to objective information, supported by studies and research. When politicians make decisions based primarily on emotions and personal beliefs rather than objective facts, they end up in a mess of ideological thinking. Make no mistake, the emotional aspect is even present in science. The evaluation process itself is also subject to strict control aspects. Reliability is not only an empirical postulate, but also a moral responsibility that applies to everyone.

The sources of the professional investigations highlight the complexities within global political dynamics, such as the shift from existential concerns to geopolitical rivalries, the clash of world powers and the emergence of unconventional leadership styles. In evaluation, more and more attention is paid to what happens between the lines, where anger, annoyance, envy, indignation, hostility and irrationality are additionally hidden. The uncertain knowledge about the settings disrupts the planned interactions externally. The competitiveness of performance is increasingly coming to the fore. That's why it's important to accurately recognize the power potential and dynamics. Without a rating, the scope of interpretation becomes narrow.The process of evaluation itself is also subject to strict aspects of control. Reliability is not only an empirical postulate, but also a moral responsibility that applies to all.

In politics there are tipping points, similar to those in natural sciences, which are irreversible, at least for the moment. Once such point has been reached, it can be difficult or impossible to reverse the changes that have been set in motion. The aim must therefore be to avoid reaching such tipping points at all. Of course, it would be best to take precautions and not let things get to that point - society needs to be warned early in order to adapt to situations that are unwanted.

Effective communication, transparency and collaboration are essential in providing early warnings and ensuring that the public is aware of potential risks. By fostering a culture of resilience and preparedness, leaders can help empower individuals and communities to take proactive steps to mitigate risks and adapt to changing circumstances. Risk factors for society include political carelessness and negligence. That's why it is important for political leaders to carefully consider their decisions and actions, as they can have far-reaching consequences that are difficult to reverse. Wrong decisions exacerbate humanitarian crises, particularly if they fuel conflict or limit support for vulnerable populations. Public perception plays a role when negative decisions are discussed in the media and cause lasting damage to the specific image. Political instability, conflicts and rampant competition between political parties can lead to government collapses and economic uncertainty, reducing investment and growth. However, political stability achieved through oppression or lack of competition can also breed nepotism and complacency. Negligence in addressing human rights issues is a growing concern, with major sourcing countries like China, India, Vietnam, and Mexico registering higher risks of modern slavery. Businesses face increasing legal and reputational challenges due to human rights abuses in their supply chain.

Fakes and disinformation are deliberately used as weapons in the information war to manipulate and divide public opinion. Platforms such as TikTok, Facebook, Twitter and Instagram provide ideal conditions for the dissemination of disinformation, because they enable manipulated content to spread quickly and widely. These platforms are especially vulnerable to fakes since they focus on fast and visually appealing content, that is often shared without verification. The mechanisms behind this targeted disinformation are multifaceted. Manipulated content is often created by state actors, government-affiliated groups or even individuals. The goal is to promote specific narratives, sow distrust, and deepen societal divisions. For example, fake news spread through manipulated videos of triumphant military victories can evoke emotions such as anger and fear, thereby strengthening support for certain political or military actions.

Extremist politicians who knowingly spread false political information online and support extremist groups must be held accountable for their actions. Several studies have shown significant links between spreading false information, advocating extremism and inciting aggressive political behavior. The impact of disinformation is significant. This leads to a distorted perception of reality and can impact decision-making at both the individual and societal level. It can greatly influence public opinion. In addition, such fakes undermine trust in traditional media and official sources of information, making it increasingly difficult for people to distinguish between real and fake news.

Combating this form of war propaganda requires several approaches. Above all, media literacy is crucial. The public must be able to think critically and verify the authenticity of information. Secondly, technological solutions are necessary to detect and curb the spread of disinformation. Algorithms and AI-based tools can help identify and flag fake content. Thirdly, international cooperation is needed to develop and implement common standards and strategies to combat disinformation.

Fakes and disinformation in information warfare pose a serious threat. A conscious and informed approach to media, along with increased efforts in education and prevention, is essential to counter the spread of fakes and maintain the integrity of the information scenery. The importance of professional policy evaluation in modern governance cannot be overemphasized. It is an important tool to ensure that government actions are effective, efficient and aligned with long-term goals and priorities. By balancing interests, power and influencing factors, the legitimacy of a policy is increased and the needs and concerns of all those involved are taken into account. Evaluations are part of sound public administration and contribute to promoting public accountability, learning and increasing the effectiveness of the public sector through improved decision-making.

The policy stimulus following positive progress will be crucial to ensuring that a society remains on the path of change and growth. By continually working toward policy change, a society achieves long-term, sustainable progress. Security guarantees should not only focus on individual components but should ensure the security of the entire system. This means that the different parts of a system, which go beyond national objectives, must interact and work together to ensure comprehensive security.

The power of country groups plays a decisive role in international politics. Entities with more power and greater interests tend to have a strong influence in the world. Trade relations, investments and economic development stimulate international relations. Military strength and the ability to deploy it, determine their status. The ability to maintain diplomatic relations and form alliances with other parts of the world influences the mutual strength. Current global trends and important events, such as terrorism, migration, climate change, pandemics or defense and security have their impact on political decisions.

Engagement in world politics requires a holistic approach, that takes into account the interconnectedness of global problems. By addressing issues such as social justice, human rights and humanitarian assistance in a comprehensive and coordinated manner, governments should work towards a more peaceful, prosperous and sustainable world. In political debates, models and counter-models are used to represent different ideologies, approaches and value systems. Only by comparing and contrasting these models, political actors can make reflected decisions about which approach best meets their goals and values. In an economic policy context for example, a model based on market economy principles could be contrasted with a counter-model based on social democratic principles. The free market model emphasizes the role of individual freedom and market forces in promoting economic growth, while the social democratic model prioritizes social welfare and government intervention to promote equality and social justice. For example, proponents of the free market model might argue that it leads to greater efficiency and innovation, while opponents point to the potential to increase income inequality and undermine social cohesion. In politics, these models are evaluated based on their perceived strengths and weaknesses, as well as their potential impact on various interest groups.

The choice between different models and counter-models depends on a variety of factors, including political ideology, practical considerations and the specific context, in which policy decisions are made. By engaging in thoughtful and informed debates, political actors make decisions that reflect their values and priorities and serve the interests of their constituents. A code of conduct is just one part of a broader strategy, which also includes measures to monitor, report and sanction violations, as well as promote training and awareness.

It is important not only to listen, but also to act accordingly. By using methodical instruments the motivations and goals of the various actors can be better recorded. A holistic approach enables the evaluation of directions and developments in politics and the appropriate reactions. The search for solutions undoubtedly plays the principle role in international relations. In times characterized by complexity, it is essential for experts, professionals and the civil society to work together developing and implementing innovative ideas. The speed and variety of societal expressions are of great importance, as they offer a wide range of perspectives and opinions that must be considered in the search for solutions. New system concepts emerge, then it becomes apparent that politics is not a personal end in itself but rather a process. The integration of various societal voices and viewpoints is paramount in the search for comprehensive solutions, providing first-hand expertise based on real-world experiences, trialing innovative approaches to societal challenges. This collaborative approach acknowledges that politics is not an end in itself but rather a dynamic process aimed at addressing societal needs.

In democracies, effective politicians must adeptly navigate this complex process and collaborate with others to achieve their objectives. The emergence of new system concepts influences significantly the political configuration, introducing novel perspectives on governance and decision-making. In essence, politics transcends individual ambitions, requiring skillful negotiation and cooperation to address multifaceted challenges and advance collective interests. As new ideas and systems evolve, they contribute to shaping the dynamic nature of political discourse and policy formulation. Thus, successful political leadership hinges on embracing this process-oriented approach, demanding inclusive dialogue and adapting to evolve societal needs and aspirations. General democracy focuses on sovereign self-determination in well-defined units, semi-presidential democracy combines presidential and parliamentary elements to balance executive powers, and supranational democracy divides authority across large regions to address collective needs and challenges beyond national borders.

A process-oriented approach is about prioritizing the steps and methods to achieve goals and not just focusing on the end results. This way of thinking is beneficial in various contexts, including individual development in politics, efficiency, and all creative endeavors. Political judgments and decisions require the ability to communicate complex issues precisely and clearly. Language skills are essential not only for effective communication, but also for the cognitive understanding of situations. In international politics, language serves as the most important tool for communicating political goals, convincing interest groups and maintaining the reputation of one's own politics. Therefore, a high level of language competence is the basis for political maturity and judgment.

International decisions do not arise in a vacuum, but through the engagement and efforts of people actively working towards positive change. The searching intellect plays a central role in helping to find new ways to tackle complex problems and create sustainable solutions. Think tanks take a methodical approach to developing practical solutions to political and social problems. They support decision-makers in planning well-founded and strategically oriented measures. These are observation methods that include political science data analysis. In order to be able to react to changes in a timely manner, continuous monitoring of developments and trends is a prerequisite. Both qualitative and quantitative methods expand comprehensive understanding. By creating typologies and models, complex issues are systematized and structured. Through comparative analysis and the identification of analogies, similarities and differences are to be highlighted and insights gained from similar cases. From this, the analysts develop scenarios and models to predict the effects of measures. Strategic planning, which includes both short- and long-term measures, is based on scientifically gained knowledge. There is always the danger that an excessive emphasis on emotional intelligence ignores the rationality of action. This could lead to inadequate control of policy and weaken the ability to respond appropriately to undesirable developments. Therefore, policy makers have to maintain a balance between emotional intelligence and rational analysis. That is why they cannot withdraw and remain silent.

The international conceptualization relies on various factors. These are economic aspects, social dynamics, historical contexts and legal framework conditions. Also the postulates of financial policy cannot be overlooked. Governments need to consider how they raise and spend taxes. Who gets what and why? Added to this are the effects of market forces on employment, prices and economic growth. International trade is subject to its own rules. Demographic developments, public opinion and social movements still play a role. Let's think about the aging population, migration trends or the power of movements like „Black Lives Matter".

A look at history often explains why actual things are the way they are. Past decisions with their long-term effects, historical conflicts with their solutions and the development of existing institutions shape the current political climate. Learning from past successes and failures provides important insights for decision-making. Constitutions establish fundamental principles, laws establish rules and court decisions establish precedents. International laws and treaties define the standards that countries must adhere to.

Formalism argues that international relations are characterized by intergovernmental cooperation and compliance with international rules and institutions. It emphasizes the importance of treaties, agreements and norms in resolving conflicts and promoting peaceful cooperation between states. In contrast, the realist approach argues that international relations are characterized by power dynamics and security concerns.

Both approaches can help to understand the complex interaction between states in the international space and show possible paths to conflict resolution and cooperation. However, both approaches share the assumption that there is no overarching authority in the international system that ensures order. States and alliances must therefore rely on self-help strategies to secure their existence. Even though neorealism sees itself as a systemic theory, while classical realism analyzes the foreign policy of states, both focus on security interests and power politics. Overall, the differences predominate: the formalist approach is strongly theoretical and abstract, while the realist approach is more practice-oriented and sees governments as central actors. What both approaches have in common is that they see insecurity and anarchy in the international system as a clear threat and use them as a central driving force.

In the international relations the significance of

interdisciplinarity cannot be overstated. The dynamic nature of global interactions demands a multifaceted approach that draws on diverse fields of study. International relations encompass political, economic, social, cultural, psychological and environmental factors. Global challenges such as climate change, terrorism, economic inequality and pandemics are complex and multifaceted. Addressing these issues effectively requires the combined expertise of various disciplines, supporting innovative solutions that a single-discipline perspective might miss. Exposure to multiple disciplines enhances critical thinking and analytical skills. Scholars and practitioners can draw on diverse methodologies and theoretical frameworks, leading to more robust analyses and better-informed policy recommendations. Efficiency must consider a range of factors including economic impact, social dynamics, legal frameworks and environmental consequences. Interdisciplinary teams can develop more comprehensive and sustainable policies.

The world political stage is constantly changing in the context of international relations. The absence of global positive strategic competition as a structuring element in international politics has led to significant change. In the past, failure to establish new political orders often led to wars and instability. The current phase reflects a similar pattern, as the dissolution of established power structures creates uncertainty. The rise of multipolarity, in which multiple nations exert influence, stands in sharp contrast to previous unipolarity dominated by Western powers, particularly the United States. This transition brings challenges as governments navigate their interests in a less predictable environment.

In the future too, it will be necessary to demonstrate strength in security thinking, otherwise credibility will falter on many levels. The innovation and research potential as well as the economic power of the entire social system depends on this. It is important to invest in security infrastructure and technologies to ensure the protection of people, businesses and state property. At the same time, care must be taken to ensure that security measures are consistent with the protection of fundamental rights. To stay one step ahead of new threats, is essential for governments to continually update their security. Ultimately, security must be viewed as a strategic priority and not an afterthought. By prioritizing security, we can build trust in our systems and protect the integrity of our societies in the face of evolving threats. Only if we show strength in security thinking, can a safe and successful future be guaranteed for everyone.

In order to make clear statements in international politics, transparency, simplicity and directness must be given priority. Political statements should be free of ambiguity or hidden intentions and communicated clearly and unambiguously. They should be based on facts and evidence, not on emotions or personal opinions. Search results underline the importance of clear statements in international politics. Leaders should choose their words carefully to accurately convey their intentions and positions and to avoid any room for confusion or misunderstanding. In an interconnected world where a country's actions can have far-reaching consequences, the importance of clarity in stating cannot be overemphasized. It should be a matter of course for politicians to continually review and adapt their international communication strategies.These principles aim to promote a more informed and engaged electorate, enhance the accountability of public officials, and improve the overall quality of democratic governance.

C. POLITICAL WORLD CLUSTERS

Which geographical clusters influence the world order nowadays? Eight geographical focal points throw their cards into the international play: 1) The Arab region forms a ring with the Near and Middle East. 2) The Pacific-Indian Circle borders it, followed by 3) the conglomerate in Southeast Asia. 4) In the north, north-east, the North Asian continent and China form their own reservoir. 5) Japan, South Korea and Australia are solid antipodes of their own style of political socialization. 6) Latin-America enters the spectrum of interests from the south and extends further north. 7) The USA and Canada represent a solid bastion and have a historically close connection to the 8) increasingly consolidated Europe. Interpolarity manifests itself in numerous alliances that overlap in many places. These clusters influence the world order by representing their own political priorities and interests.

They are forming alliances that sometimes overlap and shape the world order.

Globalization may even bring Middle Eastern people, at least the rational ones, together in expanded interconnectedness and awareness, which could lead to a greater sense of global citizenship and advocacy for human rights and democracy. The spread of information and communication technologies allows people to connect with each other and with the outside world, enabling the exchange of ideas and the mobilization of collective action against dark policies. The economic changes brought about by globalization are helping to challenge the traditional balance of power in the regions.

A multinational economy and foreign investment can lead to economic liberalization and increased competition, pushing governments to adapt to changing global dynamics. Then they also have to respond to their population's demands for more rights and freedoms. While authoritarian regimes still exist in the wider regions oft he Middle-East, the push for political reform and democratization becomes stronger through globalization. People are increasingly aware of their rights demanding accountability and transparency from their governments.

The Pacific-Indian Circle is becoming a key player in trade and economic partnerships, while Southeast Asia has rapidly emerged as an economic powerhouse. As the economies of the countries in Southeast Asia continue to grow, the region is becoming increasingly important in global trade and investment. These countries are all major players in the global economy and possess significant resources and capabilities. The Pacific-Indian Circle provides a platform for these countries to collaborate on economic issues, promote trade and investment and work towards common goals such as sustainable development and economic growth.

China's rise as a global power has been driven by its rapid economic growth and technological advancements. The country's Belt and Road Initiative, which aims to create a network of infrastructure and economic connections across Asia, Africa, and Europe, has expanded China's influence and presence in the global arena. In addition to economic power, China also wields significant political and military influence. The country's assertive stance on issues such as territorial disputes in the South China Sea and its growing military capabilities have raised concerns among other countries in the region and around the world.

Japan, South Korea and Australia, as counterparts to communist China, have significant influence in the region and play a crucial role in promoting peace and stability, which is less welcome for the Chinese dictatorship. They often collaborate on joint military exercises and share intelligence to address common security threats, such as

North Korea's nuclear program and China's growing military presence. These countries have strong economic ties and security partnerships with each other, as well as with countries like the United States. They also work together on regional issues such as trade, security and climate change.

Latin America adds diversity to the global political scenario, with a range of different structured governments and ideologies across the region. Countries like Brazil and Mexico are influential players in international organizations like the United Nations and the Group of 20. The region's rich cultural heritage, diverse populations and complex history make it a dynamic and important player on the global stage. Additionally, Latin America's natural resources, including minerals and agricultural products, contribute to its economic importance globally. The region's trade relationships with countries in North America, Europe and

Asia further establish its role in the international economy.

By being able to engage with a range of political systems and ideologies, the global community can gain a better understanding of Latin America's complexities and hurdles and gain inspiration for the region's successes in specific areas, such as social welfare and grassroots movements. In the upper part of the American continent, Canada and the USA play a significant geopolitical role in the global space due to their size, economic power and political influence.The transatlantic alliance has been forged through shared values, military cooperation, and economic integration. The United States and Canada have worked closely with European countries on a range of global issues, including security, trade and human rights. Intensifying economic and military cooperation with Canada holds significant potential for both sides of the Atlantic to achieve mutual benefits and advance common interests.

By deepening economic ties, Canada and Europe can improve trade flows, promote innovation and boost economic growth for both. At the military level, the strengthening of interoperability with Canada, that has been held under cover so far, can increase the effectiveness and readiness of joint military operations. By aligning strategies, sharing information and coordinating responses to security challenges, Canada and Europe enhance their collective defense capabilities and contribute to global stability. Looking forward, a deeper partnership between Canada and Europe based on shared values, principles and goals serves as a cornerstone for addressing global challenges and advancing shared goals. By working together on issues such as climate change, counterterrorism, cybersecurity and crisis response, both can leverage their respective strengths and expertise to make a positive impact on the global stage.

Complex relationships and conflicts arise between the individual clusters, significantly shaping global politics. It is remarkable how global power dynamics are changing and new actors are emerging on the stage. The US has long played a dominant role, but now other countries are coming into focus. China is often seen as the biggest riser, with its growing economy and political influence not only in its own region. India, with its large population and economic strength, is also among the strong rising clowds in the international arena. Brazil, Mexico, Nigeria, Indonesia and Turkey complete the picture of outstanding players in the future world order. It is expected that regional blocs will be formed, competing for influence and power. It remains to be seen which countries will ultimately take on dominant roles. The world order is in flux, and traditional power dynamics are shifting continuously. It will be exciting to see how the dynamics between the various actors will evolve.

Many of the countries mentioned pursue a confident and independent foreign policy, that increasingly emancipates itself from the "West". This trend argues that the West has promoted in former times a false conception of freedom, democracy and human rights. A new „russian exceptionalism" in turn, states that Russia has undergone its own civilizational development that differs from that of the West. However, it forgets that the greatest russian cultural potentials flourished, when the western lifestyle was incorporated and there were large economic and cultural cooperations. Longings for a Greater Russia or a Greater Serbia, on the other hand, have always brought misfortune and cost countless lives.

However, the trend towards distancing from the free West, has recently been disguised with a supposedly false idea of democracy and human rights..Because the design that the West imposes its own values and norms on other countries instead of respecting their unique cultural and historical contexts is no longer true. Historical wounds and mistrust can still make negotiations difficult. On the other hand, there are also countries that continue to orient themselves closely to the West and prioritize their relationships with Western nations. This is evident in their foreign policy decisions towards Western alliances and partnerships. These countries believe in the values of freedom, democracy and human rights and consider these to be essential to their own progress and development.

The debate over whether to align with the West or pursue an opposite foreign policy is complex and ongoing. Each country must consider its own history, values and interests in making such decisions. The key is to strike a balance between maintaining independence and cooperating with the global community to ensure peace, stability and prosperity for all. The human right to peace is not just an abstract ideal, but a practical necessity for creating a world, in which everyone can live in dignity, security and freedom. It is the foundation on which fair, equal and peaceful societies are built and which ensures that all people can lead fulfilling lives without fear and oppression.

Security, in the context of the human right to peace, goes beyond physical security and includes emotional and psychological well-being, creating stable and peaceful environments, in which individuals can thrive without constant fear of harm or instability. We need the freedom to drink clean water and breathe pure air, we want to be able to express our opinions freely and protect the free right to self-determination and self-defense, and yet we know that to achieve this we must fight against tyrannies and oppression of all kinds. That is the European credo.

For all of these tasks, the efficiency of personnel assessments in politics is increasingly seen as a crucial factor in the effectiveness of governance. Analyzing political personalities requires a combination of psychological expertise, political knowledge and strategic intuition. While structural factors such as economic interests, geopolitical realities and historical connections play a major role, the influence of the personalities of those who sit at the levers of power cannot be underestimated. Personalities have a significant influence on the direction of international politics, because they are in a position to exacerbate or defuse crises.

When we look at all the figures like Vladimir Putin, Xi Jinping, Recep Tayyip Erdoğan, Bashar al-Assad, etc., it raises significant concerns about the future of global political leadership. When we review the situation, we wonder how the political leadership of the people could look like in the future to meet global challenges. Should the question just be casually put aside? Focusing on building robust democratic institutions at international levels could help counter authoritarian trends. This includes independent judiciaries, a free press and strong civil society organizations, promoting transparency, accountability and acceptance the rule of law, as well as ensuring that political power is not concentrated in the hands of a few. Encouraging leadership development programs, that emphasize ethical governance, transparency and accountability, could help cultivate a new generation of leaders better equipped to tackle global challenges.

Assessment centers, such as practiced in companies, could play a specialized but increasingly important role in international politics, particularly in the areas of leadership selection and skills development for decision-making. Their primary role is to assess and develop the competencies of personalities, who will assume critical roles in international affairs, including diplomacy, security and multilateral negotiations.

But what are the characteristics of a charismatic leadership personality? A variety of characteristics come into play, such as emotional intelligence, leadership style, willingness to take risks, ideology and personal beliefs. These characteristics impact the way political leaders overcome challenges and seize opportunities. Leaders in international politics should be able to translate complex geopolitical contexts into understandable narratives and get people excited about their ideas. Such a talent is particularly valuable when there is a need to make decisive decisions and take responsibility for them. Those who have the potential to inspire people and bring about positive change must not forget that these same abilities can lead to polarization and conflict, if not used with wisdom and responsibility. Their influence must always be viewed in the context of structural factors and institutional framework conditions.

Charisma is also useful where unpleasant things have to be decided out of the necessity of the circumstances, which does not necessarily make you popular among the general public, but certainly increases your reputation as a leader. Some things have to be done because they are necessary. But because you don't find the change pleasant, usually the decision is postponed as long as possible into the future. Political players have to recognize that changes are necessary. But who likes change, whih i soften uncomfortable, tiring and challenging. Therefore, it is decided to perfect the ingenious strategy of "wait and see and drink tea" because "society is not yet mature enough for change".

Who needs rational thinking and well-considered decisions? Instead, methods such as gut feeling and reading coffee grounds are preferred. Together, those responsible are celebrating a state in which standing still is considered the highest form of creativity. Because if you don't do anything, you can't do anything wrong! It is true that decision-making in politics depends on the intellectual maturity of society. Making fun of the rational approach would not have a positive impact on the maturity level.

Is the endless wait for maturity just a social game of patience? After all, the art of procrastination is deeply rooted in the human DNA. It's much more exciting to ignore the seriousness of the situation and make fun of it. How much more exciting it is to put immaturity on display and see how long things can be delayed before everything collapses. Such world political heroes appeared particularly during the times of military support for Ukraine, and then quickly declared themselves as the great sages of peace. The maturity of the audience – what a concept for politicians to play around with! But who wants to be mature? That sounds more like responsibility and - just not - like reason. The need can wait - after all, we have all the time in the world! What comes out of this can be seen in war disaster areas such as Ukraine. What else will happen to us in the world?

The Russian president's leadership style has often been described as authoritarian, with a strong focus on restoring Russia's influence. His professional career in the KGB, his rise to power, and his strategic use of resources, explain his inherent tendencies to influence world politics. Political actions such as the annexation of Crimea in 2014 and military interventions in Syria and Ukraine have increased tensions between Russia and the West. These measures challenge international norms. The Russian government has been accused of disinformation campaigns and cyber operations aimed at undermining democratic processes in other countries, particularly during elections. This behavior has raised concerns about the influence of foreign powers on domestic politics. The consolidation of power and the suppression of dissent within Russia has implications for international perceptions of human rights and democracy. This behavior has an impact on the international perception of human rights and democracy.

A slightly different expression of international incomprehension is the style of President Trump in the USA, who prefers tough negotiating tactics, often accompanied by threats and public pressure, and even as president puts himself above the law. His politics are based on populist themes and he uses mass communication to mobilize his followers and attack opponents. He does not shy away from aggressive confrontations and often uses polarizing rhetoric. Many analyzes highlight Trump's narcissistic tendencies, his need for self-admiration, and his low tolerance for criticism. Authoritarian rulers advance so quickly, precisely because the mass of the mob is initially so small, that it is easy to fall into the trap. The behaviors of political leaders like Vladimir Putin and Donald Trump have significant implications for both, international relations and their domestic politics. One should have known and been able to prove what makes a former KGB agent tick or how an overestimating business shark would behave. Trump can only "do Trump" by frequently using insults and derogatory language to demean opponents and critics. This tactic is designed to collect followers and dominate media coverage.

It would be interesting to read a political psychogram of Chinese leader Xi Jinping, which has already been difficult to study in the past due to his questionable morals towards his parents. He pursues an authoritarian leadership style based on a strong centralization of power. He has shown himself to be a determined and often ruthless leader, willing to take decisive action to achieve his goals. A central aspect of his ideology is the "Chinese Rebirth" or "Chinese Dream," which aims to strengthen China as a global superpower. This is evident in his tough attitude towards political opponents and his rigorous control over society. Xi Jinping's psychological characteristics of the leadership style have significant implications for the U.S.- China relations. His quest for global dominance and his distrust of Western powers could lead to further tensions and conflicts.

Independence, freedom and prosperity are certainly worthy goals, but they also have their price. That's why they require the courage of the political elite, the willingness to take risks and the persistence to break away from external influences and make their own decisions. This is about letting go of familiar structures and dependencies that can be associated with insecurity and discomfort. Freedom means being able to act autonomously and pursue the own beliefs without being hindered by external restrictions. However, the prerequisite for this is a sense of responsibility and the ability to reflect on one's own actions and decisions and accept their consequences.

In any case, security plays a crucial role in society, because it protects the rights and freedoms of the individual. The importance of a holistic approach cannot be overemphasized. This approach should encompass various aspects of human well-being to ensure that policymakers make informed decisions that prioritize the long-term well-being of the population and the protection of the environment. Using alternative indicators of prosperity alongside GDP is important to provide a comprehensive picture of prosperity and progress.

One must be able to draw parallels between different facts or situations in order to see similarities or connections between them. By drawing parallels we can understand complex relationships and see connections between different areas. It can help gain new insights, make predictions or develop solutions. Parallels can be drawn in various areas such as science, art, politics or everyday situations. However, it is important to ensure that parallels are based on sound information and factual arguments and are not drawn arbitrarily.

The sovereign is not the nation. This view only leads to setbacks. The relevant causality of the undesirable developments can be derived from historical findings. The sovereign should remain the people over the nation. People should be able to come together as interest groups instead of political parties, beyond narrow-minded nationalist disputes. Nationalism creates usually corruption and conflict as a principle of oppression and exploitation. It fuels the aggression of forces on the fringes of society. The harmful metastases of nationalist seeds are difficult to remove from societies. Nationalism and party hegemony harm society and its economic prospects. Accusations against the other side are constantly pushed to the point of damaging the cause. This means that nationalist politicians typically express themselves and act less according to qualitative criteria. Their toxic politics include practices characterized by inflexibility or misunderstood compromise, irrationality and division.This type of politics creates an atmosphere of hostility and alienation between political groups, making cooperation difficult and damaging a society's social capital. Toxic politics causes political discussions to become aggressive and defamatory instead of being constructive and solution-oriented.The simplistic rhetoric of nationalism undermines Europe's success. Who is still afraid of that?

Is global politics perhaps facing a period, that is dangerously unpredictable? By promoting measures to protect the environment and to combat climate change, politics ensure that the economy remains sustainable for future generations. Investments in renewable energy, sustainable infrastructure and green technologies create new job opportunities and drive innovation. Promoting diversity and inclusivity in decision-making processes will help prevent the negative effects of nationalism and political partisanship. When policy discussions involve only a small group of people, important voices and perspectives are overlooked, resulting in decisions that do not fully address the needs and concerns of the majority. This can result in policies that are less effective or even harmful to certain segments of the population. By creating a more inclusive dialogue and recognizing the importance of diverse perspectives, policy-makers can develop more effective and equitable solutions that genuinely serve the needs of the population.

D. EUROPE IN THE WORLDWIDE POLITICAL SCENE

The European Union stands as a unique and powerful entity in the global political landscape. Comprising 27 member states, the EU has developed into a formidable force that not only coordinates policies and legislation within its borders but also influences global affairs. Through its three major institutions – the European Commission, the European Parliament and the European Council – the EU shapes policies that have an impact far beyond its borders. Its role in addressing international issues such as climate change, security, trade and development is vital underscoring the EU's importance as a global player. These institutions work in tandem to maintain a cohesive approach to governance, enabling the EU to speak with one voice on the international stage. This unity is crucial in ensuring that Europe's political and economic interests are protected and promoted globally.

Because of its economic strength, political unity and commitment to multilateralism the EU is ready to play a decisive role in world politics. As global challenges become more complex, the need for a strong, united Europe is more evident than ever. Whether it is leading on climate change, promoting global security or advancing fair trade practices, the EU's actions will have a significant impact on the future of international relations. Europe as an political entity is immediately beginning to have exactly the dimensions to achieve unity. It is neither too big to be grandiose nor too small to bury itself in an inferiority complex. The reference to Europe's historical cultural greatness and the horrors it has faced, underscores the complex and multifaceted nature of the continent's past. Europe's rich cultural heritage and history of conflicts and tragedies have shaped its identity and provide a backdrop for its current efforts towards unity and cooperation.

If chaos were to emerge in some areas of the European continent, this could lead to a situation in which a variety of complex problems would disrupt the European social order.This can have various causes, such as political instability in some authoritarian states, economic crises, social tensions or migration flows. All of this can lead to uncertainty, unrest and an uncertain future. The lack of common solutions or an interrupted cooperation between European entities would make things worse. The effects are diverse, such as political divisions, economic downturns, social unrest or the weakening of European integration. Political divisions can worsen, creating an environment in which populism and nationalism thrive, increasing polarization between member countries and undermining democratic norms. Economic downturns could arise from fragmented policies that hinder trade and investment, slowing down recovery from crises and exacerbating existing inequalities. Social unrest could arise as citizens become disillusioned with their governments' inability to address pressing issues, leading to protests and popular discontent. If trust in institutions weakens, the social fabric of European societies could collapse, fostering divisions along ethnic lines or ideologies.

It may also have global implications, as Europe plays an important role in international politics and economics. The situational behavior applies to all of European citizens. An economic downturn affects not only single workers directly but also their families and communities. Economic uncertainties can lead to inflation and higher living costs, reducing citizens' purchasing power and impacting their standard of living. Reduced consumer spending affects local businesses, leading to closures and further job losses. Small and medium-sized companies, which are often the backbone of local economies, are particularly vulnerable. A European economic downturn is straining public finances and leading to cuts of essential public services such as healthcare, education and social programs.

Economic problems in the EU could increasingly affect other regions of the world. This underlines the deep interconnectedness of global economies. As these economic challenges spread, they often exacerbate existing problems in other countries and create a domino effect that causes economic slowdowns, currency fluctuations and trade disruptions around the world. These economic difficulties then lead to political discontent and instability both within the EU and in other regions. Dissatisfied populations can pressure governments to make changes, which stimulates shifts in political power. The combination of economic stress and political instability creates a feedback loop that further complicates the efforts to address these issues, at both regional and global levels

When extremist movements are radicalizing, rioting and endangering democratic structures, it weakens the European Union. A weakened EU could lose its influence on the world stage, impacting not only trade relations but also geopolitical stability and the ability to address global challenges. Unrest in the EU encourages aggressive governments. When a large political and economic bloc like the EU is distracted by internal conflicts, such as left-wing or right-wing extremists coming to power, Europe would no longer be able to respond effectively to external threats. This creates opportunities for aggressive actions such as territorial expansion or interference in other countries' affairs without fear of consequences. Conspiracy theorists and those seeking to disrupt systems use these actions to advance their own unreal narratives. By spreading misinformation, sowing discord or promoting conspiracies, they destabilize international relations and weaken trust between nations.

Whether Europe could die quickly or slowly is essentially a question of its capabilities in terms of security, freedom and prosperity. The European institutions need to think about how things can be done better. The megaregion model in Europe could help to bundle initiatives. Parliamentary measures in macro-European regions would finally defeat the bureaucratic juggernaut. The unification of political Europe into larger geographical structures with similar basic interests offers an opportunity to tackle common challenges more effectively.

When the EU is preoccupied with internal issues, it is also taking part in the shift of global balance. Authoritarian regimes use this to assert their influence in regions where the EU has traditionally played a stabilizing role. This leads to increased geopolitical tensions and instability. Indirectly, this uncertainty affects global markets, trade relations and international cooperation. Fears foster an environment in which authoritarian leaders feel comfortable advancing their obscure agendas under the guise of restoring order and stability.

Since the EU is a key player in many international organizations and agreements, from climate change initiatives to security alliances like NATO, internal discord could weaken the EU's ability to act cohesively in these forums, reducing the effectiveness of international cooperation and multilateral efforts. The public in European countries might not always be acutely aware of the intricate geopolitical implications of EU unrest or how it benefits aggressors and dictators globally. Unjustified provocations by uncultured agitators and dictator worshipers, as they occur within Europe, destabilize the system of relationships in international orders. Such actions disrupt the fragile balance necessary for constructive and peaceful cooperation. Provocative rhetoric and actions leads to increased tensions, mistrust, and ultimately diplomatic and economic conflicts. Can civil society remain silent on this issue? The political management of a free world is not condemned to inaction.

It is quite paradoxical. After a time when the overarching goal of the EU was to create a seamless, cooperative and peaceful union, a far-right and far-left resurgence is now trying to weaken this framework. Citizens are confronted with a grim reality in which their sense of security is fading faster than a sandcastle at high tide. The EU, which was seen as a beacon of stability, now has internal difficulties in responding effectively to crises. It seems that the EU's current complicated mechanism, with its unanimity principle, was designed for anything but actual emergencies and reveals its weakness at the worst moments.

And what do people do when they feel the loss of

security? Of course they are more worried. But this worry is not just a mild worry, it is a deep-seated fear that permeates every aspect of life. Suddenly, the broader political environment no longer seems to be just an abstract concept discussed in newsrooms and parliamentary debates. It becomes an immediate, pressing problem that affects daily life. People are beginning to question the foundations of their political systems, and who could blame them?

The impression that only empty phrases are only being trotted out in national parliaments has led to calls for a stricter assessment of parliamentarians' qualifications. While referendums have already proposed aptitude tests, the idea often seems unrealistic. But just as managers, CEOs and other decision-makers are subject to professional assessment, similar tools should be applied to parliamentary candidates, at least at the level of the European Parliament. The inclusion of professional assessments for parliamentarians can significantly improve the electoral process and political governance. By focusing on the results of such assessments, the public can make more informed voting decisions, leading to greater efficiency in political elections. This would voters allow to base their decisions on concrete criteria rather than on rhetoric and promises. When voters have access to detailed assessments of candidates, they have a more informed choice. This would help ensure that elected representatives are competent and able to effectively represent their electorate. This is all the more true for the European Parliament with its high standards. What would European parliamentarians be, if they had only ignorance and incompetence?

In such an environment, candidates would be aware that qualifications and achievements are being reviewed, which could encourage them to take responsibilities in a more serious manner. Anyone who refuses to do this would likely earn a reputation for not wanting to do anything constructive. Coupled with a high level of motivation, there is also a high willingness to take risks that one is not so easily prepared to take. This promotes a culture of responsibility and professionalism. Reputable assessments can help mitigate the influence of populism and charismatic but unqualified candidates. Then voters will be less influenced by empty promises and emotional appeals. One could make precise and attractive offers to voters, if there is a play with open cards. Or is it difficult for some things develop in the European institutions, because civil society is not interested?

It is more than just a political experiment that shows cracks under pressure. Perhaps it is a reminder that complex regulations are not a substitute for a system that must be flexible, responsive and, above all, able to stick together for maintaining the basic security and trust of its citizens. Election results are not a dream concert. Even if they do not always correspond to the idealized ideas or wishes of the individual, they are an expression of democratic principles and values. It is important to respect their outcomes and work toward constructive engagement and dialogue to address differences and move forward as a united community.

The harsh reality of the street will not answer the big questions of asset security, financial stability and prosperity. How they are coordinated is heavily influenced by media coverage. Public sentiment inevitably depends on the factors that must be seriously evaluated for prosperity and security. It is all the more important that the media do serious and responsible work in advance. Therefore, they also need to be monitored and evaluated. The possible dissolution of structures can certainly be partly attributed to a lack of information or misinformation among the population. However, attribution of blame is a complex matter involving multiple factors and actors.

The media plays a central role in informing the public about EU affairs and has a responsibility to objectively report on EU policies, debates and decisions and to provide context and analysis that helps the public understand complex issues. If the media fails to provide accurate reporting, the public may not fully understand the issues at hand. This can lead to misunderstandings or misinformation about the EU and its role. Crossfire and cynical behavior in the European Parliament that disrupts the culture of debate and common efforts in Europe must be exposed and dealt with appropriately. Transparent media reporting can help expose such behavior and inform the public about it. Through critical reporting, media helps strengthen the accountability of policymakers and expose unconstructive behavior. This increases public pressure on political actors and encourages them to pursue more cooperative approaches. Through balanced reporting, media contribute to improving the quality of political discussions in Europe and strengthening the EU's collective efforts. A comprehensive and balanced reporting on EU affairs is essential for an informed citizenship and a well-functioning democracy. The media must strive to cover EU issues in depth, highlighting different perspectives and giving the public the tools to form their own views. Failure to do so risks leaving the public uninformed and disengaged from the EU decision-making process. However, this must also be done in a manner that is engaging and gripping. Reporting on events and issues related to the EU needs to capture the public's attention, using clear and compelling storytelling, visual aids, and relatable examples to ensure that the audience is both informed and interested.

National party leaders have sometimes used the EU as a scapegoat for domestic problems, fueling Euroscepticism and misinforming the public. The evidence suggests that EU scapegoating by national politicians is a major factor in increasing Euroscepticism across Europe. Instead of addressing legitimate domestic concerns, populist and nationalist parties have elevated their concerns to the EU level and blamed Brussels for problems that actually arose from national politics. This strategy has allowed parties to exploit public discontent and mainstream disillusionment and steer them towards opposition to European integration. However, the roots of the population's dissatisfaction lie more in unresolved domestic political issues than in the EU. Over time it has been shown that investing in EU cohesion policy actually helps reduce Euroscepticism in regions that benefit from this funding. Awareness and appreciation for the role of the EU have increased.

Humanistic European values refer to a set of principles and beliefs that emphasize the dignity and worth of the individual. They are rooted in a philosophical tradition that emphasizes human experience and rational thought. These values are often associated with the development of European thought. The belief in the inherent rights of all people, including civil, political, social and economic rights. These include the right to life, freedom of expression and equality before the law. A commitment to democratic governance in which power comes from the people and a legal framework that protects the rights and freedoms of individuals. Emphasis is placed on reason, scientific research, and critical thinking as tools for understanding the world and making informed decisions.

Ideally, de-bureaucratization in Europe takes place through a strict restructuring of the regions. Legal specialists could see this as a horror idea, because they would have to break out of rigid thought patterns. But, doing nothing in the European construct is not an option. The reputation of over-bureaucratization must be countered. This restructuring involves streamlining the decision-making processes, reducing red tape and simplifying regulations to make them more accessible and understandable for citizens and businesses. It also includes decentralizing power and giving more autonomy to local governments and communities.

Promoting innovation and digitalization will help streamline administrative processes and make public services more efficient and user-friendly. Investments in the training and skills development of officials would modernize administrations. De-bureaucratization will become a key element in making Europe more competitive and better able to respond to the needs of its citizens. By promoting cooperation across national borders, such an approach could potentially streamline decision-making processes and improve regional cooperation on common issues such as economic development, environmental sustainability and cultural exchange.

The idea of breaking down rigid thought patterns raises important questions about sovereignty, governance, and the legal implications of operating within a more fluid regional structure. A key challenge would be the need to create a legal framework that takes these newly created regions into account. This would involve reconciling existing national laws with new regional regulations and ensuring compliance with EU law.

The creation of regions as transnational administrative units in Europe holds significant potential for addressing contemporary challenges in European governance. By simplifying governance structures through larger regions, several key improvements could be achieved. The consolidation of multiple national and subnational administrative bodies into fewer, more comprehensive regional units could simplify bureaucratic structures. This would potentially reduce the time and resources spent on administrative procedures. Fewer bureaucratic layers mean that decisions can be made and implemented more quickly. This is particularly crucial in situations requiring urgent action, such as financial sanctions or crisis management. A centralized yet regionally-focused administrative framework could enhance the consistency and speed of policy implementation, ensuring that EU directives and regulations are uniformly applied and enforced.

Makro-regions span national borders and augments deeper integration and cooperation. Issues such as environmental protection, transportation, and infrastructure development often transcend national boundaries. Makro-regions could provide a platform for a more cohesive and coordinated approach to these challenges. By encouraging cross-border cooperation, makro-regions could strengthen the sense of European unity and identity. Citizens and governments alike would be more likely to view themselves as part of a larger European community. Cross-border regions could pool resources, knowledge, and expertise, leading to more innovative and effective solutions to regional issues. This collaborative approach could also mitigate regional disparities and promote balanced development.

The newly established regions span national borders and promote deeper integration and cooperation. Issues like environmental protection, transport and infrastructure development often transcend national borders. Large regions provide a platform for a more coherent and coordinated approach to addressing the challenges. By promoting cross-border cooperation, macro-regions strengthen the sense of European unity and identity. Both citizens and governments are more likely to see themselves as part of a larger European community. Border regions pool resources and expertise, which should lead to more innovative and effective solutions to regional problems.

Ensuring adequate representation within broad regions is critical to aligning local and regional interests. By giving municipalities and smaller administrative units a voice within the larger regions, local interests are better represented and taken into account. This could lead to more tailored and effective interventions that resonate with local populations. Effective representation improves communication channels between local, regional and EU authorities. This ensures that the concerns and needs of local communities are communicated upwards and taken into account in the wider decision-making processes. With optimal representation, there is a greater chance of aligning local, regional and EU-wide objectives. This could lead to a more coherent and harmonized policy that reflects the different needs and desires of European citizens.

These regions would have to identify their common challenges, goals and interests in a well-organized manner, for example in environmental issues, economic development, social issues or infrastructural aspects. All relevant actors would need to be involved in this process, including governments, local authorities, economic and social actors, NGOs and citizens. Future conferences and guided consultations help to capture the needs and perspectives of the various target groups. For a solid financing model, EU funding, national and regional budgets and also private sector investments would have to be available. Steering committees establish the coordination mechanisms that secure the procedure. The participating groups monitor progress in their networks. Since it is about our own universes in the overall European universe, effective monitoring is recommended in order to measure progress, document successful outcomes and, if necessary, make adjustments to the action plan. Transparent communication is essential for success in order to promote awareness and support among the population. The exchange of best practices between the classified regions ultimately provides valuable insights and is then summarized at a pan-European level.

The concept of large-scale regions promises to improve governance within the EU. By reducing red tape, strengthening cross-border cooperation and ensuring strong representation, such restructuring could lead to a more efficient, effective and coherent administration. However, careful planning and implementation is required to balance the interests of various stakeholders and ensure that such a structure enhances rather than complicates the existing governance framework.

Pan-European structures should be flexible enough to respond to changes and challenges. This requires a culture of adaptability and willingness to innovate within the institutions. It is crucial that European institutions such as the European Commission, the European Parliament and the Council of the European Union are strengthened to ensure effective decision-making and implementation of common policies. Europe's internal political efficiency can only be increased through clear responsibilities and responsibilities down to the smallest units.

Changing entire processes requires a lot of know-how and the necessary willingness. When situations change quickly and disruptively, it has to be done, otherwise Europe's opportunities are gone. If EU officials do not recognize that mafia state structures like Orban's government in Hungary threaten the EU and do not act accordingly, they weaken the political functionality of the continent as a whole. In some European politicians, whether in state positions or as founders of new parties, the communist spirit of past totalitarian regimes can still be felt. This poison will only be able to be removed gradually.

Policy decisions should be based on solid data and scientific evidence. Evidence-based policy uses research and evaluation results to develop and implement effective measures. Transparency and accountability include open communication about goals, measures and results. By integrating various scientific disciplines, differentiated perspectives and innovative solutions can be developed. Involving diverse stakeholders and affected communities in decision-making processes ensures that measures are appropriate and acceptable. Participatory approaches also increase the legitimacy of decisions.

Political measures should be designed for long-term and sustainable outcomes. A sustainability policy hidden by greenwashing can prove disastrous in the long term. Greenwashing describes practices in which companies or governments portray themselves as environmentally friendly without actually taking substantive measures to promote sustainability. To avoid the pitfalls of greenwashing and ensure that sustainability policies lead to meaningful and lasting outcomes, it is essential for governments and organizations to prioritize transparency, accountability, and genuine commitment to sustainability. This includes setting clear and measurable sustainability goals, regularly monitoring and reporting on progress, engaging stakeholders in decision-making processes and incorporating sustainability principles into all aspects of policy-making and operations. By consistently applying these principles, rationality in international politics can be enhanced, many mistakes can be avoided, and more effective and efficient solutions to global challenges can be developed.

Evaluation in international politics is a systematic process designed to notice the effectiveness, efficiency and relevance of policies and programs. To bringing more rationality into international politics and avoiding mistakes is a useful incentive. Evaluation begins with clearly defining the goals of a program or policy. The goals must be specific, measurable, achievable, relevant, and time-bound, Simultaneously, indicators are established to measure progress and success. Data collection follows, aiming to gather information on the implementation and outcomes of the measures. The collected data is then analyzed to evaluate the effectiveness of the measures. Various analytical techniques are applied depending on the nature of the data and the specific evaluation questions. The results and recommendations of the evaluation will be incorporated into future planning.

Streamline structural changes means create flatter organizational structures to eliminate unnecessary layers of hierarchy and reduce bureaucratic bottlenecks to promote agility and decision-making flexibility. This could be achieved by redesigning processes to eliminate redundant steps and automate manual tasks to implement e-governance initiatives to digitize services and improve transparency, while necessarily strengthening valuation controls. Implement a methodical decision-making-proces would mean to reduce time and effort required for important decisions.

It is to underline that chaos does not necessarily describe a current situation in Europe. Rather, it is a possible assumption that could be triggered by certain circumstances. It is therefore important that people in Europe work together to find common solutions to the obstacles they face. Through collaboration and co-creation, they can pool their resources and expertise to address common problems and find solutions that benefit all members in Europe. That's what increases stability and security, as well as greater economic opportunities and prosperity for all citizens.

Security policy in particular is not organized spontaneously. Systematic and comprehensive leadership is required. This includes well-trained specialists, specialized institutions and coordinated procedures to be able to respond quickly and efficiently to threats and crises. Security policies are not static; It requires continuous monitoring and adaptation to respond effectively to new threats and changing circumstances. Effective monitoring and regular evaluation of security strategies are therefore essential.

A clear and stringent leadership requires a hierarchical structure in which the responsibilities are precisely defined. Forward thinking and strategic planning are crucial in order to identify future threats and challenges at an early stage and to implement appropriate measures. Nothing should be left to chance. In this context, it must be seen how Russia's recent active measures to destabilize governments and societies have caused unpleasant irritations. Europe hast o be be vigilant and proactive in combating such tactics, which include disinformation campaigns, cyberattacks and election interference. Europe must respond to these threats in a unified manner and strengthen its resilience together. This includes investing in cybersecurity measures, intensifying cooperation between member states and working with international partners. By addressing its weaknesses and preparing for Russia's political war tactics, Europe will better protect its interests and values.

What a threat to the European continent if nationalist, populist and right-wing extremist parties gain influence across Europe. Europe has recognized that it needs to reposition itself in terms of security policy and invest more in defense capabilities in order to respond preventively to crisis situations. Politicians at least emphasize the need to prepare for new threats such as hybrid attacks, especially with regard to potential threats such as those from Russia and China.

The sale of highly sensitive technologies and military goods from European conglomerates to China can endanger the geopolitical situation in Europe in various ways. On the one hand, the transfer of technologies could lead to China further building up its military strength and potentially becoming a threat to the worlds security. In recent years, China has made significant advancements in the development of weapon systems and technologies, and acquiring know-how from Europe could accelerate China's capabilities. Furthermore, the sale of technologies and military goods to China could shift the geopolitical balance. Where is the global political commitment and compliance of some companies?

The USA and other Western countries have long viewed China as a rising military and economic power. However, if Europe sells technology and military equipment to

China, this could further strengthen China's position in the world and shift the geopolitical dynamics in China's favor. Finally, this could also trigger political tensions between Europe and other countries, especially between Europe and the USA. The US has already expressed concerns that Europe could endanger its own national security interests and international stability by transferring technology to China. Overall, the sale of highly sensitive technologies and military equipment to China should be carefully examined and regulated to ensure that it does not pose a threat to international stability.

Due to the obvious political changes around the world, the EU is taking various measures to counter the instability. This means developing a comprehensive security strategy to raise strategic awareness and improve international cooperation. It is important for the European Union to have a strong, unified voice on the international stage and to represent its interests together. This is the only way Europe can act effectively at international level and defend its values and interests. It is therefore crucial for the individual members of the Union to put their national interests aside and work for the common good of Europe.

European countries can pool their resources and expertise to address problems such as climate change, terrorism and economic instability. Destabilizers in politics, both regional and global, can be reliably identified by their actions and motivations. These entities or individuals typically exhibit several characteristics, such as ambitions for power and territory, seeking alliances with dictatorships, and the unlawful accumulation of personal wealth. Destabilizing intentions pursue aggressive foreign policies aimed at expanding influence or territory, often disregarding international norms and laws. Typical signs include efforts to dominate neighboring countries or regions through military means or economic pressure, to maintain relationships with authoritarian leaders to secure strategic advantages, to gain access to resources or gain other geopolitical influence. Relying on appeasement strategies in such cases would be disastrous.

Populist leaders who stoke nationalist sentiments and threaten EU cohesion undermine common democratic institutions. Parties or movements that oppose EU integration and have ties to Putin's Russia or other authoritarian regimes endanger peace on the continent. Attention must also be focused on major powers waging proxy wars, economic coercion and cyberwarfare to destabilize other regions or countries. Terrorist organizations and multinational criminal networks that operate across borders and undermine stability and security expand the spectrum of negativity. With a few exceptions, organized political crime mostly comes from outside to disrupt internal conditions.

How can governments reduce the likelihood of conflict? Setting up and maintaining open communication channels offers possible solutions. Before more disputes break out, there are enough opportunities through participation in regular multilateral negotiations. If information about potential threats is exchanged there, the escalation framework is checked. Observing overall geopolitical developments and analyzing them can build mutual understanding and mitigate potential damage in international politics before conflicts escalate to extremes. Whether it's through financial power or military cooperation, support can help ensure the safety and security of distant opponents. By coming together and working towards a shared vision for the future, Europe can continue to play a significant role in the global community. Europe can secure its place as a key player on the world stage.

Within the European Union, regions and countries must coordinate their efforts and work towards common goals. By supporting each other in times of need, Europeans are able to build a stronger, more resilient community. This heritage, formed in numerous defeats and victories from ancient times to the present, is an essential part of European identity. It is diverse and is reflected in numerous areas of life. Sport, culture, research, technology and business are areas in which the common values, traditions and goals of Europeans are expressed. If European regions and countries promote these elements in collaboration, they will be able to maintain and develop their common identity.

Populist and nationalist movements often try to antagonize people and question the achievements of European integration. They stir up fears and spread fear. It is about maintaining social cohesion in a political peace order with a sovereign market economy. European politicians must now reflect on the reasons behind wars and uprisings designed to weaken the West. They should have understood that these events have a direct impact on European living standards and freedom. Citizens affected by inflation, food shortages, lack of access to medicines such as those experienced during the coronavirus pandemic and potential security threats may also be considering the role of nationalist, extremist and other disruptive forces in fueling these problems.

Ultimately, it is important for voters in Europe to be aware of these indirect influences on their personal well-being and to take them into account when making voting decisions. It is necessary to combat these destabilizing forces to maintain the continent's continued prosperity and security. These include diplomatic efforts to resolve conflicts, implementing economic policies to curb inflation and strengthening security measures to protect citizens from potential threats. They just have to be efficient and to be supported by the citizens.

Strong internationally coordinated self-defense is the basis for a robust diplomacy and a strong economy. At the global level, states that have a credible defense capability are preferred to conduct diplomatic negotiations from a position of strength. This strength can deter potential attackers and facilitate peace negotiations. Self-defense is a core element of the peace ethic; it is not only justified, but absolutely necessary. Neglecting it leads to feelings of guilt, false pacifism leads to destruction.

Where is the potential to defend the free world, the power of deterrence? Is international peacekeeping still a generally recognized topic among the public? Who stays away from it? If the Europeans have not yet been able to maintain peace militarily on their own, it might one day be the case that Europe disposes of his own independent potential. The logic of fear will by no means bring long-term success. It is more courageous to convince potential opponents, that the costs of hostile actions exceed many times the alleged benefits. This idea is based on the strength, credibility and effectiveness of capabilities to forge alliances and strategic partnerships. If a freedom-loving world maintains a robust defense posture, it can deter its adversaries and prevent conflict from escalating.

Investments in military capabilities improve interoperability and coordination between allies and partners to successfully defend themselves. Deterrence is based on the principle of deterring adversaries from initiating hostile actions by demonstrating the ability, determination and willingness to respond decisively to aggression. The combination of military, diplomatic, economic and informational instruments requires absolute determination. This signals that red lines really must not be crossed. By demonstrating the ability to defend itself, the free world can deter adversaries from unleashing impetuosity. When the rules-based international order is called into question, that is reason enough to fight back.

For example, giving in to the ambitions of Putin's neo-imperial thinking would trigger a wave of copycats from other would-be dictators around the world. In addition, the proliferation of weapons of mass destruction is aggravating the world situation. What happens in these geopolitical tightropes? Are there hidden signs of a bitter ending to a story? Horror scenarios appear on the screens of political fantasies.

Economically speaking, solid self-defense supports security in investments and trade relationships. Companies and investors are more willing to invest in countries, that take their own security seriously and are actively committed to maintaining peace and stability.

The European Union should not allow itself to be influenced by fear and division, but rather embrace its diversity and unity for a more prosperous and peaceful future. Cultural heritage is a treasure that must be valued and protected, so that future generations can enjoy it. It is what defines Europe and should be a source of pride and inspiration. Diversity is a strength, not a weakness. Europe's cultural heritage is a source of inspiration and creativity, bringing people together and improving understanding. Despite all its experiences with ups and downs, Europe must preserve its common history and traditions while being open to new ideas and perspectives. Innovative solutions to this complexity can only be found by working together as a European unit. New technologies offer both, opportunities and challenges for democracy. Historical analyses shed light on how technological innovations can be used to promote citizen participation while minimizing the risks of disinformation and manipulation. Critical reflection on historical mistakes is essential in order to avoid similar mistakes in the present. For example, the economic mistakes of the Weimar Republic, which led to hyperinflation and ultimately to the Nazis coming to power, serve as a warning. However, it also provides insights into what opportunities were missed. An example of this would be the failure to include Eastern European countries in the political axes of the West after the Cold War, which is now seen as a missed opportunity and which has contributed to the current geopolitical tensions. A sad example of belated political intervention was the failure of the United Nations to prevent the genocide of the Tutsi in Rwanda in 1994, in which one billion people lost their lives. The Srebrenica massacre in the former Yugoslavia, in which an estimated 8,000 civilians were murdered by Serbian troops, can also be attributed to the UN's carelessness. The reaction came far too late. Inaction and waiting are among the deadly sins of international politics.

Why is it always the less intelligent who seriously resort to aggression? It underscores that resorting to aggression as a primary tool of foreign policy or diplomacy is often counterproductive and short-sighted and indicates a lack of wisdom or strategic thinking. Diplomatic efforts and cooperation should be more effective than aggression or conflict in resolving disputes and advancing mutual interests. In contrast, smart and effective international relations are characterized by creative diplomacy, cooperation, conflict avoidance and respect for international norms and values.

However, proactive acquiescence is not a sustainable or effective strategy for solving problems either. There are foreign ministers in Europe, almost from smaller countries, who say, that dictatorships are a fact of life that must be recognized. Such an approach exposes them as trained bureaucrats rather than dynamic political managers. This perspective reveals a worrying lack of political drive and sensitivity to critical security issues and underlines the importance of staff appraisals in the political environment of ministries. Giving up is a bad option and only makes the disaster worse. By giving in, a state signals that it is not prepared to resolve conflicts decisively. The result is further uncontrolled escalation. Compromises on security-related issues jeopardize security. This is because the threats are not adequately countered and the troublemakers are encouraged to carry out further attacks. Incidentally, a state that gives in very quickly, weakens its negotiating position. In the long term, it even loses influence and credibility in international negotiations. A one-off concession can serve as a precedent and make all future negotiations more difficult, as other opponents expect similar concessions. It happens just like in sports, if you give up too quickly in a competition, you risk that your opponent will gain self-confidence and appear more aggressive. Is it perhaps the case that there are rusty office stallions at the top of the ministries who have perhaps never had to demonstrate toughness and resilience in sport?

Another approach to important insights into world events is expressed in the understanding of history. "Those who do not look back into history have no future" is a truism that applies everywhere in the world, including in international politics. Reflecting on the past provides valuable insights that can contribute significantly to overcoming current political challenges. Studying past policy decisions and actions helps understand what worked well and what didn't. The historical perspective can help policymakers make decisions more conscientiously and informedly to avoid repeating past mistakes. Many current political issues have historical roots. Examining past events makes it possible to trace the origins of complex problems and understand their long-term effects. The study of political history reveals examples of effective governance and accountability mechanisms. It stimulates transparency in decision-making processes and strengthens public trust.

The introduction of the welfare state in many European countries after the Second World War was a response to the social and economic challenges of the time. Comprehensive social security systems were created, particularly in Germany with the social market economy and in Sweden with the welfare state model. These models created a safety net that contributed to social stability and promoted economic growth. Today, these systems are facing new challenges such as digitalization, demographic change and globalization. Historical analysis shows that adjustments and reforms are necessary to meet new conditions. For example, a universal basic income could be an answer to the loss of jobs due to automation through AI.

Only unity and solidarity enable effective European

decision-making and implementation of policies that benefit all citizens in the Union. To achieve this, the cooperation of all members is essential. A European economic and monetary union makes its contribution to strengthening stability and growth. This not only benefits individual units, but also contributes to the overall prosperity and well-being of the entire continent.

Another problem arises on a completely different level. The economic downturn across the EU highlights the importance of addressing people's concerns about financial security and well-being. As economic conditions worsen, individuals and families face greater uncertainty and hardship. This increases the urgency of effective policy measures to stabilize and stimulate economic growth. As the EU struggles with economic challenges, it may be less able to offer international economic assistance. This vacuum can be exploited by dictatorial regimes to strengthen their positions.

Governments must prioritize policies that promote job creation, support businesses and improve social safety nets to ensure the resilience and recovery of all citizens in the face of economic challenges. People care about their financial security and well-being, and the economic decline within the EU may make these issues even more pressing. Only when it has a direct impact on people's livelihoods, when jobs are lost, inflation takes over, and public services are no longer available, does the public wake up. The light at the end of the tunnel will be visible in the form of investments in sustainable technologies, promotion of innovation and education and the creation of a stable economic environment. Long-term strategies that focus on inclusion and social justice are aimed at ensuring that citizens have a better quality of life in the long term.

The list of sins of the nationalists and their classic politicians is so extensive that they cannot escape it and thus represent the root of European disunity. The classic politicians in the negative sense are characterized by the fact, that they act primarily to maintain power and benefit their party instead of working for the common good. But Europe can only be successful under common European auspices. The call for greater transparency and effectiveness in decision-making is particularly relevant at a time when many citizens feel that their voices are not being heard. Rating services for political management and civil society could help increase the efficiency and accountability of political actors.

A concise European constitution is needed to define the procedural procedures. It serves to establish the Union's institutional structures, to define the competencies of the various organs and to guarantee the fundamental rights of the peoples. A European constitution has the potential to strengthen democracy within ist borders by enhancing transparency, accountability and legitimacy and by providing clear guidelines for decision-making and the protection of fundamental rights. It could help to build a stronger and more united Europe that is committed to democratic values and principles.

The increased presence of right-wing extremists in the European Parliament could lead to a more unstable political situation in Europe and call into question EU values such as democracy, human rights and the rule of law. It is therefore important that democratic forces counter right-wing extremist tendencies and work for an open, tolerant and democratic society. Once played through, if right-wing extremists were in charge in the EU Parliament, there would be more social conflicts, the future prospect would be one with less press freedom, more dirigism, more taboos. Traces of fear will be spread.

Regardless of whether they are right-wing blocs, left-wing groups, Islamist radicalization or nationalist movements, the various forms of extremist ideologies have a fatal effect on the political landscape. It is striking that in today's society, parts of the educated classes allow themselves to be bullied by ringleaders with little education. Historically, one might assume that higher levels of education would provide a bulwark against simplistic and radical ideologies. However, the current media landscape, with its emphasis on sensationalism and clickbait, has shown that education alone is not always sufficient to counteract the pull of well-crafted extremist narratives. it also requires a portion of rational steadfastness.

Narratives have a significant impact on the mainstream by shaping the way information is perceived, interpreted and disseminated. They are not only narratives, but also powerful tools that shape social identities and influence societal structures. Narratives are structured stories that serve to convey complex information and create meaning. They help people to understand their reality and to orient themselves in social contexts. In today's world, where social media play a central role, people are not just passive consumers of narratives, but also active producers. This leads to a dynamic interaction between individual and collective narratives. Narratives have the potential to mobilize or marginalize social groups. Such polarizing narratives can be observed in many countries and how they contribute to the division of society. The mass media play a crucial role in spreading narratives. Critics note that the media often systematically spreads lies or favors certain narratives. The mainstream is thus shaped by the prevailing narratives, which often cement the status quo and support existing power structures. New narratives often emerge as a reaction to social change.

Given this threat, it is crucial to develop and implement effective strategies to combat extremism in the EU. One of the biggest challenges in dealing with extremist tendencies in the EU is the diversity of ideologies and motivations behind extremist behavior. Right-wing extremist groups propagate racism, xenophobia, and nationalism, while left-wing extremists focus on social revolution, criticism of capitalism and anti-fascism. Islamist extremists, on the other hand, rely on religious fundamentalism and violence as means to achieve their goals. This diversity of ideologies complicates the development of a unified strategy to combat extremism. The prosecution of extremist perpetrators and organizations is essential to ensure security in the EU and to contain extremist activities. Effective cooperation between the member units promoting democracy, rule of law, human rights and tolerance are fundamental values of the EU, that can help counter extremist ideologies and strengthen societal resilience against extremism. The threat of extremism in Europe, both from the left and the right, has become a pressing concern for policymakers and security experts.

Maybe we don't feel it as much on our idyllic island, but it's all around us. It means being vigilant before it's too late. Democratic values and freedom must not be endangered. It is important to stand up for diversity and democracy and to combat any form of extremism. This is the only way to maintain an open and free society. Politically motivated extremism is based on political illogic, while ideological terrorism is based on radical worldviews. Both justify hatred and violence. Furthermore, gender ideologies are partly responsible for the fact that right-wing extremist movements are gaining momentum. Values get confused or even lost. As an antidote, ingredients of diversity should be carefully mixed with a pinch of democracy. Because at the end of the day, we all want to enjoy a piece of this delicious freedom without anyone spoiling our appetite.

Clown parties and criminal groups with angry ideologies

are gaining influence through a combination of political discontent, manipulative tactics, weaknesses in democratic institutions, and global trends. Combating these phenomena therefore requires strengthening democratic processes. Measures must be taken against corruption, as well as comprehensive public education about political processes and the dangers of extremist ideologies . What does Europe's new efficiency look like? What is his excellence? The traditional political parties are no longer at the center of power. Consequently, performance and its evaluation must be transparently communicated to the population right up to the peripheries. In the context of globality, there must also be European industrialization with a focus on sustainability and innovation. Europe's excellence lies in its ability to adapt, and thrive in a rapidly changing world, with the well-being of its citizens as a top priority. This new efficiency is driven by collaboration, transparency and a commitment to continuous improvement. It's about proactively tackling global challenges, and creating a more resilient and adaptable society.

The European Union is characterized by its ability to lead by example in a constantly changing and evolving environment. Instead of dissound, unisound creates a common identity while emphasizing diversity. Purely abstract thinking about Europe is of no use to anyone. This means that a more nuanced, pragmatic approach to European integration and cooperation is needed. The personnel assessment of suitable political leadership positions is an essential prerequisite for appropriate action in the socio-political change- management. The success of political managers depends on the qualifications of their teams. The starting point for new perspectives is the consistent consideration of the system, the economic relationships and the social dynamics. The importance of creative thinking and the courage to act are incentives for the willingness to influence development. Anyone who waits and hesitates loses. A highly motivated sense of political leadership needs to be cultivated. Therefore, positions in the Commission should be filled with rationally determined and the European Council moreover with charismatic leaders.

It is important for Europe to have leaders who are visionary, proactive and willing to take risks to drive innovation and progress. By fostering a culture of courage and proactive leadership, the EU can position itself as a dynamic and forward-looking entity, driving positive change and shaping its own future. Competence and functionality make it clear that no efficient organization can function without the fourth dimension of time and therefore without control.

Political mismanagement does'nt pay off. Aimless action, also known as flying blind, contradicts the definition of competent political action. The risk escalates when the European construct clings to something that is outdated. There always has to be something moving. If too little is done, this is the worst possible outcome. The responsibility lies in the hands of the European society itself. This cannot leave individuals indifferent. A deep understanding of the European public is demanded, even if this is sometimes accompanied, by a not insignificant level of unease. The power of philosophical reflection and collective conscience should be available to do the right things in difficult situations.

Of course, people always find it difficult to make changes. But non-conflict projects are suspect, perhaps even prematurely dead, so that the best collaboration arises from the confrontation of ideas. This underlines the importance of efficiency, time management and clear goal setting in political leadership. The lack of a clear vision and an effective strategy can lead to ineffective political action and increase the risk of mismanagement and aimlessness. In the fast-paced world of politics, it is crucial to continually evolve, adapt to change. overcome Old ways of thinking should be overcome to realize a better one, which is relevant and effective. Therefore, factual disputes should be viewed as an opportunity for growth and development rather than an obstacle or problem.

With determination and united efforts, the European Union can take a strong and independent position in the world. It is of the utmost importance that all the peoples of Europe recognize the urgency of the situation and are prepared to support the necessary changes. Only by acting together can Europe secure its future and play a positive role in the global order. Europe is at a crossroads. Threats from authoritarian regimes are increasing and a new geopolitical field of tension is emerging, characterized not only by military conflicts but also by economic, energy and technological rivalries. In order to survive in this new world order, Europeans must wake up and realize that a fundamental change in their structures is necessary.

Europe's dependence on external energy sources, particularly from countries with authoritarian regimes, represents a significant vulnerability. Recent geopolitical tensions have shown how vulnerable Europe is due to its energy dependence. It is essential for Europe to build a sustainable and independent energy supply. This can be achieved through the expanded development of renewable energies such as solar, wind and hydro power, as well as through the diversification of energy sources. Simultaneously, investments in research and development of new technologies like hydrogen and battery storage must be promoted. These steps are not only ecologically sensible but also strategically necessary to ensure Europe's political and economic independence.

The economy is the backbone of any society. For Europe, it is crucial to build a strong and independent economy that is globally competitive and resilient to external shocks. Promoting local production and reducing dependence on global supply chains are central strategies in this regard. This means that Europe must realign its industrial policy and increasingly rely on domestic resources and production capacities. Additionally, deeper economic integration and cooperation within the EU is required. Only through a joint and coordinated effort member states are able to tackle economic tasks and strengthen their position in the global market. Investments in future technologies such as artificial intelligence or biotechnology are also essential to assume innovation leadership.

E. CHANGE MAKER IN INTERNATIONAL POLITICS

The need for internal European unity is evident in the response to external challenges. Following the Russian attack on Ukraine, the EU budget was used to provide emergency aid and support. This shows how important a united Europe is in order to be able to respond to unforeseen global crises. Furthermore, Europe faces the task of keeping pace with the US and China in key areas such as digital transformation. Without a coordinated approach and pooled resources, the EU risks falling behind here. Financing the reconstruction plan through joint bonds and new EU own resources such as a digital tax or CO2 border levy is another example of how greater integration can increase Europe's ability to act. These measures make the EU more independent of contributions from individual member states and therefore more flexible in times of crisis.

Once again it all boils down to the fact that it cannot function without internal unity. In no area is this more clear than in that of internal and external security. Securing Europe requires a joint defense policy. The creation of a European Defense Union, capable of operating independently of external alliances, is a necessary step. Such a union enables a rapid and coordinated response to threats and strengthens Europe's security architecture. Greater defense spending is required to acquire modern military technologies and equipment. Furthermore, Europe needs to invest in cybersecurity to protect itself from the growing threat of cyberattacks. The digital space has become a new battlefield and Europe would do well to prepare to defend its infrastructure and data.

Implementing these changes requires the support of the whole European population. Education and awareness are crucial in this context. Political education can help raise awareness of the need for reforms and mobilize support for corresponding measures. Democratic institutions and processes must be robust and resilient to authoritarian influences. Initiatives in a sense of community and solidarity among the members can help promote a unified and determined stance.

Change makers in international politics can be found wherever innovative ideas, courage to change and commitment to the common good come together. They work in governments, international organizations, civil society, the media and many other areas. Usually they possess strong negotiation skills, allowing them to negotiate agreements, build alliances and resolve conflicts on the international stage. The ability to persist in the face of adversity is important, because they often encounter significant resistance. They combine business acumen with social impact, often developing scalable models that can be replicated globally. Universities and think tanks house scholars and researchers, who contribute to global discourse, influence policy through their work and educate future change-makers. Some change-makers work within or lead NGOs focused on global issues such as human rights, environmental protection and poverty alleviation. These organizations often have international reach and collaborate with governments and other stakeholders to drive policy changes. But where can they be found and who is it in Europe?

European change-makers have significantly shaped the continent's political, economic, and social landscape, leaving an indelible mark through their leadership and initiatives. Ursula von der Leyen, as the President of the European Commission, stands out for her pivotal role in shaping European policies, particularly on critical issues such as climate change. Her leadership in advancing the European Green Deal exemplifies her commitment to a sustainable future for Europe. Similarly, French President Emmanuel Macron has positioned himself as a key advocate for a more integrated and stronger European Union. His efforts to reform EU institutions, promote multilateralism, and address global challenges like climate change and migration have cemented his status as a significant personality in both European and international politics. In the realm of security, Jens Stoltenberg, the Secretary-General of NATO, has been instrumental in navigating the alliance through complex challenges, including Russian aggression in Ukraine. His leadership in adapting NATO's strategy to address new security threats and in strengthening transatlantic ties has been crucial during a time of heightened global tensions.In the business sector, Paul Polman, the former CEO of Unilever, has been a leading advocate for sustainable business practices and corporate social responsibility. Polman's efforts have been pivotal in promoting the idea, that businesses can and should play a central role in solving global challenges, such as climate change and poverty, demonstrating how corporate leadership can intersect with social impact. Beyond individual achievements, several European institutions have also been distinguished by the accomplishments of their personnel. The European University Institute in Florence is a prominent academic institution focusing on European studies, political science, law, and economics. Scholars from the EUI have consistently contributed to policy discussions in Europe and beyond, influencing international relations and governance. Another key institution is Bruegel, a leading European think tank specializing in economics. Bruegel provides valuable research and policy recommendations on global economic governance, trade, and financial stability, influencing both European and international economic policies with its rigorous analysis. The European Investment Bank based in Luxembourg, plays a critical role in financing projects that promote European integration, sustainable development, and social cohesion. The EIB's investments often have a significant social impact, contributing to the economic and social fabric of Europe and extending its influence beyond the continent. Lastly, the Munich Security Conference, MSC, holds a unique place in international relations. Its special feature is that talks and discussions take place outside the strict diplomatic and protocol requirements, allowing participants to speak openly and directly about global security issues ranging from military conflicts to terrorism, cybersecurity, and climate change. The MSC is well-known not only as a forum for exchanging ideas and strategies but also as a venue for important negotiations and bilateral talks that often set the course for future international policies. In summary, European change-makers, whether individuals or institutions, have played and continue to play a critical role in shaping global policies and addressing the complex challenges of our time. Their contributions underscore Europe's ongoing influence in the world.

If an uncoordinated and still dominant rhetoric does not change, the policy will fail. Many people have their own everyday problems and concerns that require their full attention. But when personal matters take center stage, international politics often gets neglected. Another reason could be a lack of interest in politics in general. Some may prefer perfecting their avocado toast recipes or watching the latest cat videos on YouTube to consuming political information. Who needs political information when you can watch funny memes instead? The lack of interest in what is happening in Europe and the world can have various reasons, such as a lack of trust in politics, a feeling of powerlessness or insensitivity to political decision-making processes. Many young people feel that EU policy is too far removed from their own reality.

Despite the importance of the European Parliament as the only directly elected supranational body, voters do not see any significant improvement in its democratic legitimacy. But they need the problem-solving of complex problems such as refugees, youth unemployment, energy policy, environmental protection and global threats. Relative prosperity, health and peace, in short, the european future is at stake if the European community does not fight the difficulties. This can only be achieved together, not through individual actions. Natural disasters are felt all over the world, earthquakes, droughts, hunger, water shortages and they come suddenly, as the technical term goes, disruptive.

And to make matters worse, wars and attacks from all sides on human rights freedom are increasing. Europe as a whole must not proceed ideologically but rather idealisticall focusing on promoting unity, cooperation, and progress for all its member countries. By embracing an idealistic approach, Europe can work toward common goals and values that benefit all its citizens, rather than getting bogged down in individual ideological differences. This can help create a stronger, more cohesive European Union that can tackle the challenges together with all members.

European politicians have to uphold democratic values, defend human rights and strengthen the rule of law. They must counter disinformation, protect electoral systems and promote transparency in decision-making. It is important for citizens to remain vigilant, informed and engaged in the political process to safeguard democracy and the European project for future generations. Where will Europe be in the year 2040? This could already be predictable by the year 2030. Independence, freedom and prosperity come at a price. Europe is expected to find itself in a significantly different geopolitical environment in 2040.

Perhaps then the United States may have lost its position as a leading world power, while emerging countries such as China or India gain influence. This could lead to new alliances and violent conflicts. Europe itself may continue to face economic challenges such as an aging population, a shortage of skilled workers and the consequences of climate change. The EU should nevertheless develop and play a stronger role in international affairs. But at the same time, Europe's independence and prosperity are threatened by populist movements, terrorism and cyberattacks. It is therefore still important for Europe to work closely together and find common solutions to these challenges. The tasks ahead are pretty clear on the table. Key priorities include Europe's security and defense capabilities, economic growth and innovation, addressing climate change and environmental threats and migration control. A frozen democracy system that is increasingly influenced by lobbyists or extremist deniers of reality weakens the existential systemic process.

Analyzing European politics in the context of the European elections and the common future in the face of emerging global unrest is undoubtedly a remarkable topic. The electoral mood barometer often overlooks the influence of the media and political propaganda on voters' decision-making. Voters are influenced by biased or misleading information spread by political parties and media, which can distort their perceptions and ultimately their voting decisions.

The emotional and psychological factors that play a role in the run-up to an election are often underestimated. Afraid of the future, anger and frustration can all play an important role in shaping voters' decisions, leading them to make impulsive or irrational decisions at the ballot box. European elections are crucial for the Union's democracy and have an impact on the public's political orientation and decision-making. They reflect the political mood and concerns of citizens in the various member states. In times of increasing global uncertainty such as geopolitical tensions, economic challenges, climate change and technological changes, the EU is under great strain. European countries can only act effectively together. They face complex problems that require a coordinated response.

EU members – whether they will ultimately be provided by nations is another question – need to strengthen their cooperation to put common strategies on the agenda in areas such as climate protection, trade, security and technology development. European elections are an important act of European civil society to determine the future and direction of the continent. By taking part in the elections, citizens can help strengthen democracy in the EU and ensure that their voice is heard. It is important to take the EU elections seriously and not simply dismiss them as a protest election or a sideshow, as the EU institutions play a dominant role in various policy areas such as economy, environment, security and foreign policy. The decisions made in the European Parliament have a direct impact on the daily lives of citizens in Europe's smallest units, the municipalities.

Therefore, it is important to learn about the candidates and their political programs in order to make an informed decision. A careful mix of ingredients such as diversity of rationality coupled with a pinch of democracy would be a recipe for strengthening the European project. In times of extremism, it is important that Europeans stick together and ensure that their social cake remains colorful and, above all, extremely tasty.

Politically uneducated people often have difficulty understanding complex news and issues. Nevertheless, they go to the polls without sufficient knowledge. But of course everyone has the opportunity to educate themselves, although - who has endless leisure and access to unbiased information? In these terribly dense times full of disinformation and fake news, staying informed is more important than ever. After all, wading through a sea of misleading headlines and outright lies is a small price to pay for a functioning democracy.

What does European politics mean? Only if European priorities are recognized the interests of smaller European units can be met. If it doesn't work on a small scale, it will be difficult to conceive it on a large scale. No matter how small Europe may be in its units, as a whole it has wealth, value and economic potential, that must be preserved. If some of the signs are not good, they need to be shaped even more. Just like when players on a football team are sick, it's a bad sign. This is addressed by striving for recovery and changing strategies. If politics feel comfortable staying sick, they will fail.

If business and industry want to keep up with the times,

the political systems must also adapt. The EU is a sui generis construction, that differs significantly from that of the United States of America. In order to prevent the destructive two-chamber dilemma, it is possible in Europe to advance to another meta-level, namely that of macro-regions. In any case, the established regions should strengthen, optimize and maintain communication channels to the smallest units, the municipalities. This is the best way to promote safety and sustainability. Networking cooperation at regional and global levels ensures the legitimacy of the European organization. The small units therefore play a significant role in the overall concept and help ensure that the interests and needs of all stakeholders are taken into account.

In any case, the regions envisaged should strengthen, optimize and maintain communication channels to the smallest units, the municipalities. Europe also faces the challenge of keeping pace with the US and China in key areas such as digital transformation. Without a coordinated approach and pooled resources, the EU otherwise risks falling behind. Financing the reconstruction plan through joint bonds and new EU own resources such as a digital tax or CO_2 border levy is another example of how greater integration can increase Europe's ability to act. These measures make the EU more independent of contributions from individual member states and therefore more flexible in times of crisis.

As the innovative regional concept aims to streamline administration, the creation of newly formed units will reduce bureaucracy. Such a restructuring could help to overcome several challenges. By reducing bureaucracy, decision-making processes are accelerated and the implementation of political measures can be carried out more efficiently. Large regions that transcend national borders could promote greater cooperation and integration between the restructured members of the EU and enable a more unified approach to common challenges. Ensuring that municipalities and smaller administrative units are well represented in the assembled regions would improve the flow of information and align local interests with broader regional and EU-wide objectives. This bottom-up approach ensures that local voices are mirrored and integrated into the decision-making process.

Society must not allow itself to be misled by sensationalist media reports. They are merely aimed at provocation and scandalization. Instead, it should encourage itself to critically scrutinize the decisions that are made. Sensational reporting attracts more users, which means that even serious formats tend to focus on scandalous or extreme content. Established news organizations can also come under pressure to sensationalize their reporting in order to remain competitive. Once again, it is advisable to use the tools of evaluation to assess the quality and integrity of the information provided.*) Pragmatism and honesty can be helpful in many situations, especially when it comes to solving specific difficulties quickly and effectively. However, it is important not to lose sight of the long-term effects. Instead, a balanced perspective that takes into account both short-term needs and long-term goals is preferable.

Neutrality is perhaps the most clear expression of powerlessness, a seal of approval for fear and even for the absence of deeper understanding and insight, as it often means not taking a clear stance or assuming responsibility. From a philosophical point of view, it is a useless game of hiding from reality, a fig leaf for

*) „Evaluieren in Wirtschaft – Poltiik - Institutionen und Medien"
   ("Evaluation in Economics – Politics – Institutions and Media")
   ISBN 9783756228805

supposed protection, as an attempt to be fair to all sides, unsuitable for problem-solving. Sometimes it would be wiser and beneficial to society to have a clear opinion and stand by it instead of remaining neutral.

Who wants the European project to be destroyed? If right-wing extremists were in charge in the European Parliament, it would lead to a terrible mix of political drama and comedy. Imagine hardliners trying to express their views in a room full of diversity - it could lead to some pretty bizarre situations. Perhaps they would try to pass so absurd laws that they would seem more like a skit from a comedy show. Whatever the case, the dominance of extremists in the European Parliament would have serious consequences for the political profile and values that Europe stands for.

Far-right extremists generally advocate nationalist and isolationist policies that could undermine the EU's goal of promoting peace, solidarity and cooperation between its member states. They could also seek to dismantle key EU institutions and agreements such as the Schengen area or the single market, which would have economic and social repercussions for the entire Union. Civil society must not stand idly by while values and freedoms are threatened. Europe must work together to strengthen its defense both militarily and economically. Europe must invest in renewable energy sources and reduce its dependence on fossil fuels. Economic relations with authoritarian regimes must be reconsidered and alliances with other democracies must be given priority.

The extreme right propagates war, the extreme left is not much better propagating world revolution. Ultimately they both find themselves on the street. If left to the mob, chaos and lawlessness will flood every nook and cranny, all the way up to Capito, Washington. How is society civilized? The civilization of a society depends on the active participation of its members. If society is able to promote the rule of law, education, social justice, community and peaceful conflict resolution, it can counter the challenges of chaos and lawlessness. It is an ongoing process that requires commitment and collaboration to ensure that the values of a civilized society are embedded in all aspects of life.

Encouraging participation in democratic processes helps people feel more invested in the system and less likely to turn to radical alternatives. Holding leaders and institutions accountable for their actions can help maintain public trust and prevent the erosion of democratic norms. Platforms in the social media can work to limit the spread of harmful and extremist content while still respecting free speech principles. By implementing these strategies, society can work towards maintaining civility and order in the face of extreme political ideologies. It's important to remember that this is an ongoing process that requires consistent effort and adaptation to evolving challenges.

Even if many people are dissatisfied with politics, this does not justify turning to grotesque ideologies. Instead, the focus should be on strengthening democracy that promotes compelling values. This is the only way a society can exist in the long term in which everyone feels safe and valued. Democracy fatigue and the resulting susceptibility to extremist ideologies are complex phenomena, that cannot be traced back to a single cause. Instead, several factors are at play, including a lack of political education, the inability to distance oneself from extremists and the search for simple answers to complex problems. Civic education increases critical thinking skills and enables individuals to analyze information, question sources and understand the nuances of political issues. Without these skills, people are more susceptible to simplistic and extremist narratives. Extremist groups often use social influence and peer pressure to attract and retain members.

Today's demagogues are in many ways similar to the manipulators of the Nazi era with infamous names like Goebbels or Himmler. They also rely on simplistic slogans, hateful rhetoric and the claim that they have the only solution. They use various means to influence and control the masses, specifically targeting emotions and resentments. They paint a picture of a community that can only be saved through radical measures. Complex problems are reduced to simple enemy images and scapegoats. A black and white "us versus them" logic emerges. Today, as yesterday, demagogues use mass events, symbols and media to spread their messages and create an atmosphere of dangerous enthusiasm. They seek to centralize their power and suppress all opposition. Party, program and leading figure merge into one. In order to counteract this danger, disinformation and manipulation must be identified at an early stage. Simply convincingly clarifying the facts can counteract the false arguments and develop a positive vision for the future. This is the only way to effectively prevent the rise of despotism. Who wants to close themselves off to this or who can do anything else?

Later, when it's too late, it's not easy to say something different, when you have the knife at your throat. It becomes an understandable but inexcusable excuse. Because the question cannot be avoided, why does it get to the point where the knife is at the throat? This question distinguishes free, resilient people like those in Ukraine from others who mentally accept everything. It also poses the question of how the well-off people of Europe might behave in such a situation. Many European societies seem to remain in a state of contentment and prosperity. Decades of peace and economic progress have led to a comfort zone where existential threats often seem abstract and distant. This contentment can lead to a certain lethargy and lack of vigilance when it comes to defending freedom rights. To meet the challenges of the present and future, a shift in thinking is required. An active and engaged civil society ready to stand up for its rights is essential. The well-off people of Europe must recognize that freedom is not a given but must be constantly defended and re-earned.

While some in society struggle with the pesky details of reality, others have developed the remarkable ability to simply ignore anything that doesn't fit into their preconceived notions. When someone comes along with the latest scientific findings or political analysis, just put their imaginary earplugs in their ears and loudly chant "La la la, I can't hear you!" That's one of the ways to avoid being disturbed by the unpleasant truths for the time being. For them, facts are overrated. Who needs evidence when you have a strong opinion? A good ignorer knows that it's much easier to focus on what social media has to say - after all, the internet is the only place where every jackass is an expert. After all, when your favorite influencer says something, that's the only truth that matters.

An important aspect of ignoring is selective perception. When someone says that despotism is on the rise, many people simply look the other way and act as if they are interested in the latest songs in music history. It's amazing how many problems disappear when you simply listen in a different direction. After all, it's much easier to retreat into your own little world than to deal with the challenges of reality. The universe will take care of the rest. Cheers to ignorance.

The tendency of people with limited intellectual perspectives to oppose economic progress is spreading. The glorification of screaming at the fairs of uncivilized consumerism, on the other hand, is a powerful incentive for strict dictatorships to put a moral hat on their territory. Western civil society is not entirely innocent of this either. No wonder if the reaction to this degenerates into attacks and threats.

A well-functioning democracy relies on the active participation of its citizens, and at the heart of this participation lies the act of voting. However, for voting to truly reflect the will and best interests of the people, it must be informed. An electorate equipped with knowledge about candidates, policies, and issues is fundamental to the health of a democracy. Conversely, when voters are uninformed or misinformed, the very essence of democratic governance is at risk.

Uninformed voters are more susceptible to the influence of misleading campaigns, false information, and emotional appeals, leading to decisions that may not be in their best interest. When voters feel overwhelmed by the complexity of political issues or distrustful of the information available, they may become apathetic, leading to lower voter turnout and a weakened democratic process. If a significant portion of the electorate votes without adequate knowledge, the resulting election outcomes may not truly reflect the will of the people, undermining the legitimacy of the democratic process.

The deliberate spread of false or misleading information, particularly through social media, creates echo chambers where biased views are reinforced. The difficulty in distinguishing credible sources from unreliable ones exacerbates this issue, leading to widespread confusion. Cognitive biases can skew how information is processed, with voters often relying on emotional appeals rather than facts. This tendency to favor information that confirms existing beliefs further distorts the decision-making process. Politicians or media outlets may present incomplete or distorted information, with sensationalism often taking precedence over substance. The lack of accountability for false statements in political discourse erodes trust in the system. Ensuring that voters are well-informed is a shared responsibility, falling on both the "professionalists"—including the media, experts, and politicians—and the voters themselves.

Professionalists must actively engage in fact-checking and correcting misinformation to prevent the spread of falsehoods. Creating platforms for meaningful debates and discussions helps voters understand different perspectives and make more informed decisions. Encouraging media literacy and critical thinking skills among the public is essential for discerning fact from fiction in the information they encounter.

Voters must view being informed as a civic duty,

recognizing that their decisions at the ballot box have far-reaching consequences. They should actively seek out diverse and reliable sources of information to ensure they have a well-rounded understanding of the issues at hand. Engaging in respectful political discussions with others can help voters refine their understanding and consider multiple viewpoints. Enhancing civic education in schools and for adults can equip citizens with the knowledge and skills necessary to participate effectively in the democratic process. Independent, non-partisan fact-checking organizations play a vital role in maintaining the integrity of information, and their support is crucial. Using technology to make accurate information more accessible can empower voters to stay informed, even in the face of time constraints and information overload.

Skills acquired through training in any field enable learners to analyze problems and make informed decisions. This becomes even more important if a meaningful dialogue is to be held to solve social, economic, political and ecological problems. Poverty, crime and pollution are often the result of political decisions that lack critical thinking and care on both sides of the social spectrum. Education is becoming an important driver of change and ensures that economic practices are reviewed and revised for their sustainability. The transition to a knowledge-based economy has made education an essential factor for individual and social progress. Today's education systems essentially provide high-quality skills to meet the demands of increasingly specialized professions.

Individuals who lack strong political convictions or a clear understanding of democratic values may find it difficult to resist insidious influences. The rise of social media has led to the creation of echo chambers where individuals are only exposed to information that reinforces their existing beliefs. This prevents people from distancing themselves from extremist ideologies and considering alternative viewpoints. During times of economic hardship or social change, people may look for simple explanations for their problems. Extremist ideologies offer these simple, if misguided, propositions to complex problems, making them attractive to those who feel insecure or disenfranchised. It shows intellectual immaturity and ignorance to get carried away by reckless arguments. Immature people who are still developing their identities are vulnerable to ideologies. Extremist groups exploit this vulnerability by providing a sense of community without individuals fully understanding the implications. This provides a false sense of purpose and belonging that can be very appealing to those struggling with their identity.Encouraging dialogue and engagement within communities can help bridge divides and reduce the appeal of extremist groups. Creating spaces for open discussion allows individuals to voice their concerns and find common ground. By encouraging critical thinking, providing support, and strengthening social ties, individuals find a genuine sense of purpose, reducing the appeal of extremist groups. This approach not only aids in the healthy development of personal identity but also contributes to the overall stability and safety of society. If forward-looking ideas do not find a majority, it is less due to a lack of furiosity in communication than to the behavior of a civil society, that doesn't know what it wants.

Trusting those who thrive on chaos can lead to societal instability and disorder, undermining the foundations of a structured and peaceful community. Established norms and values can be eroded, resulting in a loss of social cohesion and increased conflict. Those who support oppressive regimes or ideologies often prioritize their power over individual rights, leading to widespread human rights abuses. Freedoms such as freedom of speech, assembly and the press are restricted, and dissenting opinions and critical thinking are suppressed. Those who thrive on chaos often lack the skills or intention to manage resources effectively, leading to economic mismanagement and decline. Oppressive regimes tend to create an environment of corruption that further weakens economic growth and the fair distribution of resources. Who needs freedom when you have the power to oppress others? Repressive regimes and ideologies are the true heroes of chaos. They bring order by suppressing dissent and critical thinking. After all, it is much easier to create a homogeneous society in which everyone thinks and acts alike - this is the real key to a harmonious life, or is it something else?

The increase of extremist parties on the political stage in Europe in recent years is a concerning phenomenon. Both left and right-wing groups have pursued a Europe-hostile agenda based on nationalist and anti-globalist ideologies. Left parties often view the EU as an instrument of the capitalist system that exacerbates social inequality and neglects the interests of the working class. They therefore call for a profound revolution in European institutions to limit the power of economic issues and promote social justice. At the opposite pole, right-wing extremist parties have portrayed Europe as a threat to national identity and sovereignty. They argue that the EU limits national self-determination and neglects the interests of European citizens in favor of a federal structure. Both sides have tried to exploit growing discontent with the political elite and increasing globalization to spread their anti-European messages. They have used populist rhetoric to stoke fears and prejudices among the population and provoked divisions between European countries and citizens.

China and Russia have an interest in a weakened Europe because it furthers their own geopolitical goals. China wants to expand its political and economic power in

Europe, while Russia seeks to divide and weaken European countries in order to strengthen its influence in the region. It is therefore extremely important for Europe to remain vigilant and stand together in the fight against extremist parties and anti-European forces. Only a strong European Union can guarantee the sovereignty and security goals of the continent and successfully counter external and internal threats.

When military experts say, that President Putin will be fully capable of attacking NATO countries as early as 2029, it is quite naive, if one keeps calm and excludes the possibility of such an assumption. The overall defense and security strategy must take into account the potential for hostile actions from repressive systems. Proactive measures must be taken to prevent such aggression. It would be a dangerous mistake to ignore the warnings of military and political experts and assume that such a threat is not credible. Nevertheless, Russian President

Putin seems to fear NATO less than his own people, who are striving for freedom. What happened in 2004 during the „Orange Revolution" on the Maidan in Kiev, Putin fears could also happen on the Moscow River. The revolution in Ukraine was seen as an example of the population's desire for democratic reforms and rejection of authoritarian governments.

Through a close coordination in the military area, the EU wants to create a safer and more peaceful world. Support from external partners, such as NATO, is useful to ensure common security and defense. There is potential for cooperation and complementarity between the EU and NATO to address common threats. Repression on the political stage is often the motivation for positive forces to come together. Without the Soviet Union's expansionist efforts, there would never have been a NATO in history. Without the blockade of Berlin in 1948, without the defeat of Hungary in 1956 and the suppression of the "Prague Spring" in 1968, NATO would not exist in its current form. Without Putin's acts of aggression, there would have been no resurgence of NATO. The choice between slavery and freedom, as seen by the great European Adenauer, is becoming increasingly important today.

But the European dilemma, characterized by political, economic and social problems, has led to increasing uncertainty. The situation highlights the hurdles Europe faces: economic uncertainty, the immigration and refugee crisis, the emergence of threats from populist and nationalist movements, the impact of climate change with more frequent extreme weather events and the need to transition to a more sustainable economy. In foreign relations, the European Parliament has identified key problems such as food insecurity, great power competition in Africa and human rights violations by private companies. In addition, Russia's active measures to destabilize governments and societies are a huge disruptive factor. It emphasizes that Europe must address its weaknesses and understand the attacks that Russia's political war tactics entail.

In response to the growing threat from authoritarian regimes, Europe can take various measures. First, Europe must strengthen its unity and cooperation in order to respond effectively to common challenges. This includes building a more coherent defense and security strategy and increasing investment in technology and innovation to remain competitive globally. Europe must focus on diversifying its energy sources and reducing dependence on authoritarian regimes for energy supplies. This will be achieved by investing in renewable energy sources and promoting energy efficiency. It is crucial for European peoples to understand the importance of defending their values, freedoms and democracy in the face of authoritarian threats. This calls for greater awareness, unity and action to advance a secure and prosperous future for Europe.

There are several actions that Europe can take in response to the growing threats from authoritarian regimes. Firstly, Europe must strengthen its unity and cooperation to effectively respond to common challenges. This includes building a more cohesive defense and security strategy, as well as increasing investment in technology and innovation to stay ahead in the global competition. Europe must focus on diversifying its energy sources and reducing dependence on authoritarian regimes for energy supply. This can be achieved by investing in renewable energy sources and promoting energy efficiency.It is crucial for European peoples to understand the importance of defending their values, freedoms, and democracy in the face of authoritarian threats. This requires increased awareness, unity, and action to ensure a safe and prosperous future for Europe. It is crucial for European peoples to understand the importance of defending their values, freedoms, and democracy in the face of authoritarian threats. This requires increased awareness, unity and action to ensure a safe and prosperous future for Europe.

Foreign policy, and especially international politics clearly have a lot to do with sustainability, not just on a global scale, but implicitly for each individual political entity. Citizens should therefore take the opportunity to educate themselves about international affairs and support candidates and parties that they believe pursue a responsible and forward-looking foreign policy. With their vote at the ballot box, they share responsibility for ensuring that their countries remain successful and sustainable in a globalized world.

Open dialogue and a willingness to listen to different points of view are crucial for a democratic and inclusive society. In a globalized world characterized by different opinions and perspectives, it is important to build bridges of understanding and find common solutions. This means listening respectfully, seeking evidence and facts and focusing on common goals. Promoting education, critical thinking and media literacy are key aspects of empowering people to make informed decisions and actively participate in shaping their communities. By equipping people with the skills to critically evaluate information sources, resist misinformation and meaningfully engage in public discourse, media literacy initiatives play an essential role in upholding the integrity of information and promoting transparency in media consumption.

Politically motivated extremism is based on extremist political illogic, while ideological terrorism is also driven by radical beliefs that justify hatred and violence. "What is communicable and where does one give up?" refers to the ability to communicate information, ideas or feelings in a way that can be understood by others. Even in the USA, conspiracy theorists who rebel against reality are not only found among the right-wing extremists. In the Democratic Party, the left-wing extremist fringe is at least as busy working on dismantling the world order.

How to respond to such attacks on society? The phrase "Where does one give up?" can have different meanings depending on the context. Giving up, means not being able to solve a task or having no hope of success. You can also give up if you don't want to make any further attempts or want to withdraw from a situation. The question " Where should one give up in international politics?" depends on when political actors give up their efforts or negotiations in a particular area or on a particular issue. By giving in to intimidation, countries risk undermining their sovereignty, compromising their national interests and setting a dangerous precedent for future interactions. It also erodes trust, escalates tensions and leads to a cycle of retaliatory actions that deep negative consequences for global stability and security. Surrender is an unacceptable attitude in international politics because it weakens sovereignty, security and any negotiating position. Instead, political leaders should rely on strategic and proactive diplomacy to protect their interests and promote international stability. Through principles-based negotiations, strengthening bargaining power, long-term strategic planning, internal resilience and the promotion of international norms, the political players respond effectively to the challenges and consolidate their position.

Essential diplomatic dialogue in negotiations and treaties allows to communicate interests and negotiate agreements. Diplomacy facilitates the resolution of disputes, as long as they have not reached the final stage of a conflict. International norms and standards, such as human rights and environmental policies are central areas, where communication plays its significant role. The art of diplomacy must be effective long before conflict occurs. The military conflict itself is the responsibility of military performance. Only then will it be the task of diplomacy to bring about an acceptable solution. Mediator groups can advocate for global compliance with human rights standards and also hold conflict parties accountable. The demands are similar when communicating about global environmental issues, climate change or international agreements. An important aspect is cultural exchange, often referred to as soft power. Nations use cultural diplomacy to promote mutual understanding and influence. Last but not least, economic and trade relations benefit from clearly managed communication exchanges.

However, the exciting world of diplomacy does not avoid conflicts by ignoring approaching bad weather clouds for a long time - until it is too late. Or is it the federal governments that are to blame because of their know-it-all attitude when a wrong decision is made despite numerous concrete signals? "It was all just a misunderstanding" is the excuse when things are delayed until they explode. Then it's easy to say that you didn't see it coming. So there are plenty of missed opportunities due to inexcusable decisions. "Why deal with unpleasant topics like political tensions when you can chat about the weather or economics in politics and diplomacy instead?" After all, the best diplomacy might be the one that simply ignores reality. "Tensions between countries? We haven't heard anything!" It is the last word of a perfect comedy, if it were not for the sadness of the suffering of an entire people and the threat to a continent.

The outbreak of the war in Ukraine in 2014, followed by the escalation in 2022, is the result of a complex mixture of political, historical, economic and social factors that had long been on the horizon and had been deliberately overlooked. What were the mistakes? Why were Russia's ambitions underestimated? Russia's ambition to "gather Russian soil" was already known before the Georgian war in 2008, but was not taken seriously enough. These mistakes illustrate the complexity of situations and the need for a more comprehensive understanding of political dynamics and processes. It is high time for politics at the level of the 21st century to finally introduce strict control mechanisms to assess situations and the quality of political personnel "hic et nunc", „here and now". After all, it were the seeds of a traditional political mentality that placed bureaucratic feeling above political management capacity. When will the will to reform prevail? In a modern Europe, there would be an opportunity to change the mode to future-oriented action and thinking. Will it be seized? The more proactive and coordinated responses are yet to come.

When the conflict is finally in full swing, diplomacy wants to become active again - this time to find an "acceptable solution". These solutions are usually so vague that no one really knows what they mean. "Let's just get everyone around the table and find a compromise". - That doesn't really work for anyone. This is the quintessence of wrong decisions: everyone is unhappy, but everyone wants to save face. It is one of the concrete points at which philosophy touches politics.

Despite the importance of communication, there are a number of factors that can limit its effectiveness. National interests and sovereignty usually give rise to conflicting interests that are not easily reconciled through dialogue, such as territorial disputes. Countries initially resist external influence on issues they see as core aspects of their sovereignty. Ideological differences, for example between political systems such as democracies versus authoritarian regimes or cultural values, are also high hurdles for a mutual understanding. Distrust and security concerns stemming from historical hostilities require a rethink. The lack of transparency caused by secrecy only hinders the open dialogue.

Propaganda and misinformation, including disinformation campaigns and media manipulation, disturb international information sharing. Intractable conflicts, particularly those rooted in deep ethnic or religious divisions, may not be resolved through dialogue alone. Situations in which agreement is viewed as undesirable by those involved lead to a stalemate. While sustained diplomatic efforts are critical, there are cases where traditional communication channels need to be reevaluated or supplemented with other strategies.

Persistent non-cooperation, where one party consistently refuses to engage in good faith, requires alternative courses of action, including sanctions or international arbitration. If the dialogue reaches an impasse, it will be necessary to change the strategy, such as bringing in new mediators, examining back-channel communication or applying international pressure through coalitions.

Dealing with religiously fanatical formations such as Hezbollah, Hamas, the Houthis or theocratic states such as Iran is an enormous challenge. Iran's unique blend of radical Islamism, state-sponsored terrorism and geopolitical expansionist ambitions poses incalculable provocations to global security and stability. The ideology of the Islamic Republic has profound implications that extend far beyond its borders and spill over into the Middle East and the wider international community. Addressing this threat requires a multifaceted approach that includes diplomatic efforts, economic sanctions or international cooperation to mitigate destabilizing activities and promote a more stable and secure global environment.

These formations and states often operate under deeply entrenched ideological frameworks that defy traditional diplomatic and negotiation techniques. When dialogue and peace talks are not enough, additional strategies must be employed to manage the complex dynamics. Analysts and negotiators should be well versed in the historical, cultural and theological underpinnings because informal and discreet channels of communication often lead to outcomes that are not possible in formal talks. Such back channels build trust and open up lines of dialogue that eventually lead to more formal negotiations. The provision of humanitarian and development aid demonstrates the good will to improve the lives of people in conflict areas. This could make the groups more amenable to dialogue. Targeted sanctions against resistant leaders will put the environment under pressure. The combination of diplomatic isolation with the promise of economic incentives for cooperation should bring success.

Regional big powers may have a vested interest in resolving local conflicts. For example, involving Saudi Arabia, Turkey or Egypt in mediation could increase its legitimacy and effectiveness in the wider region. First, the socio-economic grievances must be addressed. Poverty, lack of education and unemployment fuel the radicalization of extremist ideologies. Long-term peacebuilding requires a comprehensive reconciliation process, that eliminates the misunderstandings of the past.

The multiplicity of conflicts for example in Iraq or the Iranian nuclear program, pose a serious task for all players in world politics. Even if the EU is perceived as less influential compared to the USA, its role as a mediator in the background cannot be ignored. The armed conflicts, particularly in the Near-East, have led to massive flows of refugees, which have at least severely affected Europe. The currently realistic starting point for the EU is to provide humanitarian aid in these areas and to control its own borders. Europe is concerned about terrorism, migration and geopolitical tensions. Military cooperation, arms supplies and joint security initiatives could one day therefore be an important aspects of European policy. In any case, Europe must not slip into the position of influencing, but rather into the role of sustained observation and mediation.

Other geopolitical tensions, such as those in regions of West Africa and the Sahel, also affect European security strategy. Political instability and the expansion of Islamist terrorism in these areas represent a threat that requires intensive international cooperation. These missions already exist to support the security forces on site. The ideological circle of the global struggle closes here again, just to mention the Sahel, Mali or Bukina Faso. As armed conflicts increasingly exacerbate the already chaotic situation, the influence of the United Nations is shrinking, while that of Russia is increasingly growing.

Human rights and freedom on the one hand, tyranny and oppression on the other, form a background of confrontation that reaches into the philosophical and therefore into the existential. Serious answers must be given. Of course makes it a difference, whether millions of people around the world die from accidents or environmental disasters, or whether they die from diseases caused by poverty or from executions and then also from wars.

At the heart of the moral and ethical mandate is the unconditional recognition of the human dignity of every individual, as every human being has the right to life, liberty and security. Although this is laid down in writing in the United Nations, in practice it has degenerated into waste paper. Furthermore, the fight against injustice and discrimination is central to ensuring a fair distribution of resources and opportunities and combating social inequality. Simply put, this requires global cooperation to fight poverty, improve healthcare and protect the climate. Education plays a key role in this by raising awareness of the positive. However, it will not be easy to reconcile universal principles of ethics and morality with cultural sensitivity. Targeted development assistance would help some countries create democratic institutions, the rule of law and a functioning civil society. Economic incentives would be linked to compliance with human rights standards.

What responsibility do citizens have in Europe for maintaining positive progress both indoors and outdoors? Active engagement begins with participation in elections. This also includes retrieving information about the various positions. Participation in public or published discussions expands the pool of political knowledge in a society. In democracies, transparency and accountability are officially demanded.

F. GUIDELINES FOR EXCELLENCE IN POLITICS

It is necessary to find out who is working on the groundwork in the world, to ensure that there are qualified, ethical and responsible actors and organizations. When the public understands who is responsible for laws, infrastructure, education and health care, they can hold those people accountable for their actions and decisions. Potential conflicts of interest or biases must be identified. Then you also understand the opportunities that society has.

Society is certainly capable of changing things. She just needs to be guided and accompanied. From whom? It comes down to skill, experience and the right assessment by the elected and appointed management teams. Leaders with a clear, inclusive vision inspire society. Implementing measures to promote social cohesion, education and economic opportunities will help limit the appeal of extremist ideologies. Integrating capacities into education systems enables individuals to critically evaluate information and resist extremist propaganda.

Therefore, the public uses the existing media to raise awareness to the signs and dangers of extremism. Advisory and evaluation mechanisms help to recognize signs of political danger. As soon as the various elements of knowledge are combined with the necessary commitment, it is possible to control change and keep small the influence of extremism. Leaders with a clear, inclusive vision inspire society. Implementing policies to promote social cohesion, education and economic opportunities will help curb the appeal of extremist ideologies. Integrating capacity into education systems enables individuals to critically evaluate information and resist extremist propaganda. Therefore, the public uses the existing media to draw attention to the signs and dangers of extremism. Advisory and assessment mechanisms help to identify signs of political danger. When the various elements of knowledge are combined with the necessary commitment, it is possible to manage change and minimize the influence of extremism.

In a rational process, it is advisable to first examine all situations. The areas of political action are segmented and prioritized according to the urgency of the trends. Deviations from the desired course are registered and localized. This is typically the first step for political leaders, policy makers and experts in the relevant field. Consultants identify in their the critical problems and analyze data to ensure the best possible results for the projects. In addition, contributions from stakeholders, the public and other stakeholders are also taken into account.

Rationality management can be viewed as an instrument of power in international relations. The concept emerges as a way to exert power and influence in international relations. Assumptions of rationality are used to explore efficient means of achieving desirable international outcomes, for example in military strategy and deterrence. Through strategic planning and implementation of evidence-based decisions, political actors are empowered to strengthen their influence on the global stage. This includes carefully considering all available information about the most sensible course of action. By using rational measured arguments to justify political decisions, political organizations increase their credibility and acceptance of their policies among other partners.

Rationality management also serves to minimize conflicts of interest. This process is implemented through various tools and techniques such as risk assessment, scenario planning and decision frameworks. These tools enable political actors to make informed decisions based on evidence, logic and reason rather than on emotional or ideological factors. It can also help one navigate effectively in complex and unpredictable international environments. By analyzing different stories and perceiving potential outcomes, decision makers can anticipate challenges and opportunities. This proactive approach helps political actors stay one step ahead and respond effectively to changing circumstances. Where knowledge predominates, experience and intuition are required. In addition, rationality management also improves transparency and accountability in international relations. By clearly justifying their decisions based on rational analysis, political actors build trust with their partners and stakeholders.Consulting plays an important role in international politics by providing expert advice, analysis and strategic guidance to political leaders involved in global affairs. Expert advisors also help the public navigate the complexities of international relations, understand political dynamics. Counseling professionals often assist in conflict resolution, mediation and peacebuilding efforts in regions affected by political unrest or instability. By bringing together conflicting parties and providing unbiased analysis and advice, they help promote dialogue, build trust and find solutions to complex policy issues. Consultants with expertise in international relations and foreign policy play a critical role in helping organizations navigate the complexities of the global landscape, develop effective strategies for international engagement, and build successful partnerships across borders and cultures. Their skills and knowledge are essential for addressing global challenges, promoting cooperation, and advancing shared goals in the international arena.

Any meaningful strategy is based on proactive assessments and planning processes. The main objective of political departments is to promote the interests, values and policies of their respective governments. This may include advocating legislation, engaging in diplomacy, negotiating international agreements and representing interests on the global stage. To accomplish these goals, policy departments must proactively assess the policy environment, both domestically and internationally. This includes analyzing trends, identifying potential threats and opportunities, and developing strategies to address them. This includes working with other agencies, consulting with stakeholders and conducting research and analysis.

Policy departments should initiate planning processes to ensure that their tasks are implemented effectively. This includes setting measurable objectives, developing action plans, allocating resources and monitoring progress towards their objectives. Developing an effective policy requires a combination of different methods and approaches. This includes assessing policy options, their feasibility and their potential outcomes. Continuous capacity building of government officials is essential for effective policy development. Regular monitoring and evaluation of the implementation of policies is crucial for assessing their effectiveness and making necessary adjustments. This is complemented by regular professional foresight conferences and close collaboration with think tanks and qualified consultants who are committed to ensuring that policies are effective. Ultimately, it is up to the management and members of each individual institution to put these modalities into practice.

Think tanks serve as important catalysts for ideas and action and mobilize expertise to influence the policy-making process. At their best, they have the ability to stimulate the political imagination by communicating ideas, stimulating public debate and offering creative yet practical solutions. Think tanks are not evaluation agencies. Both serve different purposes and have different capacities. Futures conferences bring together experts from different fields to collaborate and brainstorm across different perspectives, leading to a more comprehensive understanding of the issues at hand. They provide valuable insights and recommendations based on research that can influence policy decisions and the public debate.

It is crucial for think-tanks that their research and recommendations are credible, independent and transparent. This includes disclosing their funding sources and ensuring the diversity of qualifications of their employees. Sometimes they have good contacts with political decision-makers. Military and political lobbyists tend to pursue specific avenues of influence. It is not good for donors' priorities to be reflected in recommendations. Therefore, the quality of the research and the underlying motivations are subject to regular review. For political rating agencies to play an objective role, they must have robust procedures and regulatory oversight. It is vital to have credibility, independence and transparency in their research and recommendations. This includes disclosing their funding sources, ensuring diversity in their staff and expertise, and maintaining a non-partisan approach. In addition, think tanks promote public debate and raise awareness of important social issues. By providing evidence-based analysis and recommendations, they inform the public and hold politicians accountable for their decisions. By examining the motivations and actions of political actors analysts are able to assess the potential implications of policy decisions and anticipate their effects on various stakeholders in the society. It involves examining the power dynamics, institutions, policies and actors that shape political decisions and outcomes. It requires critical thinking, research skills and an understanding of political theory and practice. This allows for more informed decision-making and the ability to develop strategies to address potential dangers before they arise.

Political analysis helps to uncover underlying structural issues that may be contributing to solve political instability or conflict. By identifying these root causes policymakers can work to address them in a more holistic and effective manner, rather than just treating the symptoms of a problem. Effective communication of political analysis is also important in order to inform the public, politicians and other decision makers about the complexities of political dynamics. By proactively sharing recommendations, analysts can help to shape public discourse and influence decision-making in a more constructive and informed way.

Policy managers should always stay one step ahead and deliver valuable insights and strategies to their stakeholders by staying informed about current policy trends, leveraging innovative technologies and data analytics, and drawing on best practices from around the world. This ongoing commitment to excellence and continuous improvement is necessary to address the complexities of modern politics. Anticipate and respond to challenges and opportunities. If something is simmering or even just slightly fermenting in international relations, a reaction is required.

Conflicts at international level are sometimes closely linked to the identity and self-image of the actors involved. If they see their reputation threatened, this can lead to an escalation of conflicts. In order to defuse such conflicts, it is important to understand the identities and needs of those involved and to create opportunities for social resonance. Sociometric analyses reveal power structures, alliances and tensions between actors in international politics. For example, patterns of relationships between states, governments and interest groups are documented. These findings help to better understand conflicts and develop solutions.

In today's world, characterized by often divergent opinions and perspectives, it is crucial to build bridges of understanding to find common solutions. This means listening, looking for evidence and facts and focusing on shared goals. Promoting education, critical thinking and media literacy are central aspects that enable political actors to make well-founded decisions. Education not only provides access to different perspectives, but also teaches individuals to critically evaluate information, question assumptions and engage with different viewpoints. Critical thinking skills enable the political professional to analyze complex issues, weigh evidence and make decisions based on rationality rather than on prejudice or misinformation.

Many new instruments are now available for international relations. They just have to be used skillfully. They represent the fact that we are increasingly moving away from the reactive and tackling the proactive. In order to make real progress in international relations, it is important to use these new tools in advance, i.e. to work towards long-term and sustainable solutions, to conduct preventive diplomacy and to address problems before they escalate. It is in the nature of things that problems that are solved sloppily, always arise again and again. It is the unfortunate logic of compromise. Compromises are basically just retaliatory measures.

Methods or techniques for evaluating the effectiveness of a program, project, or intervention help collect data, analyze information and make informed decisions, which are based on the results of evaluations. Political organizations can engage specialized agencies to measure the success of their programs, identify opportunities for improvement and make data-driven decisions to optimize impact and outcomes. In addition, there are assessment techniques that collect information about political actor's skills, knowledge, and personality traits. These tools help ensure accountability, transparency and continuous learning within an organization or project. The quality standard of a political unit is reflected in its performance. It is not good when political leaders, after electoral success, see themselves less as qualified politicians and more as representatives of the vote. They certainly lack the gene of managing and leading.

Media literacy is becoming increasingly important in the digital age, where information is abundant and easily accessible. Improved media literacy allows one to navigate the multitude of information sources, distinguish between reliable and unreliable sources and critically evaluate the credibility and accuracy of information. In this context, it becomes clear how important the assessment and creation of social values are.

However, there are also intrinsic elements in international politics that can hinder the effectiveness of measures, such as the use of ineffective methods, deception or psychological warfare. If leaders are unable to correct this, they should resign making room for a job rotation. Understanding the advantages and disadvantages of structures and correctly evaluating issues also means taking new risks. A lack of critical assessment of facts leads to the acceptance of misinformation. Broadly speaking, it is the basis of conspiracy theories.

The lack of adaptation manifests itself in excessive fear and paranoia and makes the individual more susceptible to conspiracy theories. Visionary backwardness leads to a limited understanding of the world; strategic backwardness manifests itself in reluctance to act. Political decision-makers are therefore morally obliged to cultivate a culture of critical thinking by focusing on the evaluation of facts and positions.

Disinterest in politics begins with the attitude "I don't care." This attitude can stem from a variety of reasons, such as feeling overwhelmed by the complexity of political issues, feelings disconnected or disempowered from the political process, or simply not seeing how politics directly affects one's daily life. Disinterest in politics has consequences for the society as a whole, as an engaged and informed citizenry is crucial for a functioning democracy. Individuals must recognize the impact politics has on their lives and the community. They must actively participate in the political process to advocate for change and hold the responsible accountable. Tackling disinterest in politics starts with opening up access to political information and removing systemic barriers. By working towards a more inclusive and participatory political system, we can help ensure that all people feel empowered to participate in the democratic process.

Using a combination of quantitative and qualitative methods can help to identify patterns and trends that might not be apparent through using only one approach. For example, quantitative data may show a correlation between a particular communication strategy and increased public engagement, while qualitative analysis can provide context and deeper insights into why that strategy was successful. By employing multiple research methods, researchers can triangulate their findings and ensure the validity and reliability of their conclusions. This can help to strengthen the overall credibility of the research and provide more robust evidence to support recommendations.

The participation of countries in international congresses can enhance the legitimacy and credibility of a government or an international organization. By observing and evaluating these events, the performance and commitment of a government can be assessed, and the results can serve as a benchmark for its effectiveness and ability. The significance of these evaluation results lies in their informative and advisory role for governments and policymakers. By analyzing the results, conclusions and recommendations can be drawn that can influence policy measures and decision-making processes. These recommendations may include suggestions for new policy initiatives or reforms based on the insights and experiences presented at the congress.

One incentive for using the combination of research methods is that it allows for a more comprehensive understanding of the overall effectiveness of congress events or crisis summit conferences. The quantitative approach provides numerical data on public perception, while the qualitative approach provides insights into the impact of communication strategies. In order to build trust in politics and overcome carelessness, it is important to promote political educationin a way, that understanding of political processes and democrac will be improved. Many people do not understand the complex political connections, which leads to a loss of trust. Political education can provide knowledge about the political system and the value of democracy, so that citizens can sharpen their judgment and participate more effectively.

Clear outlines of the specific goals and targets of certain fractions should be aligned with the overall mission and vision of a country. Than follows an evaluation of the internal strengths and weaknesses as well as the external opportunities and threats. This analysis will help identify areas where strategic initiatives can make the most impact. A detailed plan should include specific actions, responsibilities, timelines, and resources required. In a monitoring scheme the effectiveness of the strategic initiatives and their impact should ontinuously be evaluated.

Evaluations and assessments should preferably be conducted externally, as self-assessment does not meet the requirements of empirical methodology, according to the principles of social sciences such as reliability, validity, and credibility. Linguistically speaking, self-evaluation is as nonsensical as "apologizing to oneself". External evaluations by independent experts ensure a well-founded check that meets the standards of empirical research.

Consistent exaggeration undermines a nation's credibility. Once other countries recognize the pattern of overstatement, they may question the reliability of future claims, weakening the nation's negotiating power. Domestically, an inflated self-image leads to unrealistic expectations among the population. When the reality fails to match the promoted image, it results in public disillusionment and decreased trust in leadership.

One of the key advantages of observational research is its high external validity, as it provides a realistic picture of politicians behaviors and actions. Observational research also allows for the collection of rich and detailed data. Researchers can note specific behaviors, interactions, or contextual factors that may be overlooked with other methods. It provides insights into unconscious or subconscious behaviors, as well as capture non-verbal cues or body language, which may not be conveyed through surveys or interviews. However, observational research also has limitations. It can be time-consuming and require significant effort, as researchers may need to spend long periods observing and recording data. This approach allows advisors to tailor their recommendations to real policy needs. They can recognize the dynamics and patterns in the communications and interactions of political actors and thus develop more effective strategies for solving problems. When the basic interests are represented graphically, the true situation is perfectly clarified.

Scenario technology allows possible developments to be analysed. Various contingencies are created, based on different assumptions that present alternative results. A possible hypothesis could be, for example, an increase in nationalist and populist movements leading to the election of leaders who prioritize nationalism and closed borders. This suggests increased tensions between countries, trade wars and a decline in international cooperation. The other scenario involves the continuous rise of technology and globalization, leading to a more interconnected world in which traditional borders and barriers are being dismantled, leading to more cooperation and global governance. The latter ultimately contributes to a more rational strategic planning.

By exploring such differencies, policymakers and stakeholders can better understand the potential risks and opportunities that lie ahead. They can than take proactive measures to mitigate risks and capitalize on opportunities, ultimately shaping a more stable and prosperous future for their countries. The scenario analysis helps in building resilience and flexibility in policy-making, enabling decision-makers to adapt to unexpected changes and uncertainties in the political environment.

Consensus should be the preferred approach to conflict resolution or decision making. In contrast, compromises have a reputation for being harmful in the long term. It is better to be consensus-oriented than compromise-oriented. A compromise is an agreement reached through mutual concessions, where each party gives up some of their demands to find a middle ground, consensus involves working together to find a solution that satisfies the concerns of all parties as much as possible. Compromises lead to inequalities in the distribution of tasks. When one party takes more share than its legitimate, it leads to frustration and feelings of injustice. In a compromise, it will usually happen that neither party gets their preferred solution. This means that the chosen solution is not the most effective or efficient, which could cause problems in the long term. They create blockages that do not improve the situation, so there is a general lack of clear direction or accountability This in turn leads to a lack of motivation, delayed progress or even complete failure of the agreement. So, compromises are not the elixir, because they harm rationality. Their votes resemble horse trading, while the consensus would remain an agreement of reason.

The height of the irrationality of compromise is found in the theory of double circle of jurisdiction, which has been applied since the practices of the Soviet Union, nowadays supported by the current Kremlin regime and continued in some UN votings. "The arbitrary termination of contracts is inadmissible, but not every termination is in principle arbitrary and therefore not unlawful". The struggle for compromise is a fictitious one, because it leads far away from a permanent solution of the problems. If you only know the neutral reversal, you do not get far; moreover, neutrality gives despotism free rein in advance. This is exactly what right-wing extremist groups or existing dictatorships still want today.

In a pluralistic society, understanding through open dialogue, mutual respect and the willingness to learn from different perspectives is advisable. A socio-political education can play a decisive role in encouraging individuals to critically examine their own beliefs and values, as well as the beliefs and values of others. Through dialogue, decision-makers can navigate the complexities of a diverse and contradictory society by engaging in respectful and constructive conversations, making assumptions and promote empathy and understanding. It is essential to balance the importance of cultural identity with the recognition of individual rights. While cultural diversity is a source of richness and vibrancy, it should not come at the expense of the rights and freedoms of individuals. Cosmopolitan thinking can help bridge the gap between cultural diversity and individual rights by promoting a sense of global citizenship and empathy for others, regardless of their cultural background.

By fostering independent, critical and creative methods, policymakers can develop the skills needed to deal with the complex challenges of a diverse society. The aim of summit conferences or congresses must be to unlock the potential of cultural diversity and encourage participants to embrace and celebrate the richness of different perspectives. A new professional field is opening up for rating agencies in politics. With the increasing polarization and complexity of political spheres around the world, there is a growing need for unbiased and expert analysis of policies and trends. Political rating agencies could specialize in assessing the credibility, effectiveness and performance of political leaders and governments. They also provide evaluations of the proposed policies and their potential impact on various stakeholders.

The claim to shape results is a fundamental approach to achieving consensus and requires a logical foundation. To deal with a superficial issue risks succumbing to populist reactions. This requires that decisions are based on informed and rational considerations, based on a thorough analysis of the respective situation. However, when issues are approached superficially or without careful consideration, there is an increased risk of favoring simplistic or populist responses.

Populism often thrives on oversimplified portrayals of complex issues and tends to promise quick solutions that may not be sustainable or effective in the long term. Therefore, it is crucial for political decision-makers and actors to adopt a deliberate and well-founded approach to understanding complex problems and developing appropriate solutions. The legitimacy of political management in the public should not depend solely on emotions and popularity. Equations with many unknowns are not solved by emotions. Credibility is guaranteed exclusively through factual know-how and transparency. Populism lives on simple messages that reflect the frustrations and desires of the public. When a topic is not studied in depth, it is shaped in a way that is consistent with populist rhetoric and often pits the "people" against the perceived elites. Conversely, strengthening the middle class is a good recipe for launching opportunities for elite excellence.

A strong middle class usually has some degree of economic security that allows people to take risks. Any superficial analysis ignores the nuances and underlying factors that contribute to social problems and leads to misguided solutions that do not address the causes. In an age of rapid information dissemination, superficial discussions can spread quickly, reinforcing echo chambers and polarizing opinions. This environment can discourage critical thinking and differentiated debate, as individuals may be inclined to simplified explanations that are consistent with their existing beliefs.

The creation of start-ups that act as political rating agencies represents an innovative approach to improving political oversight and transparency. At a time when public trust in political institutions is declining worldwide, the need for such agencies is more urgent ever. To achieve this goal, several steps and measures must be carefully implemented. First and foremost, start-ups need to define a clear mission and specific goals. Their primary objective should be to increase transparency and accountability among politicians and political institutions. This can be achieved by assessing factors such as adherence to laws, effectiveness of political measures, freedom from corruption, and responsiveness to citizens. These criteria must be transparent and understandable to ensure public acceptance of their ratings. Independence in evaluation is crucial for the success and credibility of political rating agencies. In order to avoid conflicts of interest, they must secure financing primarily through crowdfunding, foundations or neutral organizations. Financial independence allows these agencies to work objectively and impartially.

Corruption in the context of international treaties and agreements can occur in various ways. Companies might pay bribes to government officials in order to obtain lucrative contracts for infrastructure projects, resource extraction or public services. They may attempt to influence policy and legislation through opaque lobbying practices in order to shape contracts in their favor. One example is lobbying by large pharmaceutical companies to obtain favorable terms in international trade agreements. In many resource-rich countries, international contracts for raw materials are often riddled with corruption. In other international development projects, money intended for aid may be diverted through corruption. Dictatorships may use military action to secure resources needed to maintain poweror gain strategic advantages. This can also include the suppression of dissent or uprisings in resource-rich regions. Military actions often lead to human rights abuses, including displacement, violence against civilians and the destruction of livelihoods.

To address the problems of bribery and military violence, a number of actions are needed at international level. The use of sanctions against governments and companies involved in bribery or military force to extract resources can be a deterrent. These sanctions could include trade restrictions, asset freezes or entry bans for responsible persons. Local activists and independent media play an important role in exposing corruption and abuse. Companies should be encouraged to develop ethical guidelines that focus on transparency, environmental protection and social responsibility. A combination of many measures can significantly reduce the practices of bribery and military force in raw material extraction. However, it requires continued efforts and cooperation between governments, international organizations, civil society and the private sector.

Blockchain can be used to track the origin of raw materials such as minerals, oil and gas. Each transaction is stored on a stable and transparent platform, which facilitates monitoring and reduces the possibilities of corruption and illegal trade. This can help prevent bribery and opaque financial flows. AI can identify unusual or suspicious financial transactions or contract terms that could indicate corruption. AI-based systems can analyze satellite data, social media and other data sources in real time to identify illegal activities such as unauthorized mining or deforestation and respond immediately. Satellite images and drones can be used to monitor the use of resources such as forest areas, mines or oil fields. This allows for accurate monitoring of environmental degradation and illegal activities, even in remote areas. Drones and satellites can collect evidence of human rights violations related to military operations to secure resources, and share this information with the international community. Social media can be used to raise global awareness of corruption and human rights abuses in resource-rich countries.

Platforms that make government data available allow

citizens and international organizations to monitor contracts, licenses and financial transactions, thus exposing corruption and illegal practices. Modern technologies play a central role in analyzing political data. Artificial intelligence and Big Data enable efficient processing of large volumes of information and identification of patterns that complement human analysis. These technologies can enhance the objectivity of ratings and improve the efficiency of analytical processes.

AI is a great opportunity to speed up proceedings in the legal systems. AI-powered tools can quickly analyze vast databases of legal precedents, statutes and regulations, providing lawyers with relevant case law and insights, which can expedite the research process. AI tools can streamline the process of drafting, reviewing, and managing contracts, ensuring compliance and reducing the risk of errors. While the integration of AI into the legal system presents numerous benefits, it also raises important ethical and regulatory considerations, such as ensuring fairness, transparency and accountability in decision-making processes.

The use of artificial intelligence in the context of freedom of expression and dialogue raises profound ethical and political questions, especially in an authoritarian or restrictive political system such as the People's Republic of China. If AI is used to monitor, control or suppress dissent, it has far-reaching consequences for individual freedom and social plurality. The idea that AI is dominating the military is one of the most disturbing developments being discussed in the modern world. Misguided development has the potential to become an existential threat to humanity. This is not only due to the technological capabilities themselves, but also due to the ethical, political and security implications that result from them. "Killer robots" could identify and attack targets without a human being involved in decision-making. The unpredictability and risk of error of such systems could lead to uncontrollable escalation. Who is responsible if an autonomous weapon makes a fatal mistake or causes civilian casualties? The introduction of such systems raises profound ethical questions, since it significantly limits human responsibility in war decisions.

The race of research with moral surveillance is inevitable, and where does the cultural component stay? Science doesn't care about regulations. Therefore, scientific advances require continuous ethical monitoring to consider potential impacts and consequences. This is particularly true in sensitive areas, such as new technologies or biomedical research. Every society is shaped by specific cultural values and norms that influence its view of technological developments and their ethical implications. While some cultures focus on progress and efficiency, other societies place greater emphasis on human dignity, solidarity and sustainability. The way AI and other technologies are developed and used reflects a society's ethical priorities. Different cultures may therefore have different ethical approaches, which makes it difficult to develop global ethical standards for AI. AI is inevitable, the results are not. This statement implies, that although the development and use of AI is inevitable, the concrete results and consequences of this technology depend on human decisions.

Political ethics is increasingly becoming a guiding principle in international politics. For Europe this means both, a mandate and the opportunity to exploit its potential in terms of content and technology. It is generally the demand for international transformation performance. Europe has the ability to set standards in international politics. By prioritizing political ethics, Europe can influence global norms and practices, encouraging other nations to adopt similar standards of governance and international conduct. Political ethics reinforces Europe's commitment to multilateralism and international cooperation. Upholding ethical principles in international relations can strengthen global institutions like the United Nations, the World Trade Organization, and the International Criminal Court, which are essential for addressing global challenges.

As technology plays an increasingly central role in global politics, Europe has the opportunity to lead in developing ethical standards for emerging technologies. This includes areas like artificial intelligence, data privacy, cybersecurity and digital governance, where Europe can set global benchmarks for responsible innovation.

One of the challenges Europe faces is balancing ethical considerations with the realities of global power politics. While ethical principles are important, they must be implemented in a way that is pragmatic and effective, taking into account geopolitical dynamics. Europe must be consistent in its application of political ethics to maintain credibility on the global stage. This means addressing ethical concerns not only abroad but also within Europe, such as issues related to migration, social inequality, democratic governance and supporting sustainable development goals through economic policies. Europe can advocate for reforms of global governance structures to make them more inclusive, transparent and accountable through evaluations and innovations.This includes ensuring that new technologies respect human rights, protect privacy and are accessible to all to avoid technological splitting.

Diverse and reliable data sources are essential in international politics. Political rating agencies should draw upon a wide range of information, including official government documents, media reports, academic studies and feedback from citizens. Utilizing multiple sources allows them to paint a more comprehensive and balanced picture of the political landscape. Another decisive step is collaboration with experts from political science and research institutes. Experts provide robust data analysis and research findings that inform policies. This helps in creating evidence-based strategies rather than relying on populist rhetoric or uninformed decision-making. Political scientists identify emerging trends and potential threats, allowing governments to proactively address issues before they escalate. An additional task of research institutes is also to examine social, economic and cultural factors that contribute to the rise of populist and extremist movements. Understanding these root causes is critical to developing effective interventions. Collaboration with experts allows access to a wealth of knowledge on best practices and successful interventions from around the world. It can enhance the quality of media reporting on political issues, ensuring that the public receives accurate and comprehensive information.

These partnerships validate analyzes and continually improve the agencies methods. Expert knowledge and scientific support are essential for producing informed and reliable ratings. Regular reporting and active public relations efforts are necessary to disseminate rating results and stimulate public discourse. Social media and digital platforms will offer effective and reliable channels to reach the public and promote transparency. By regularly publishing reports, political rating agencies raise awareness of their work and the importance of their mission. Citizens should be informed about the operations and significance of political rating agencies. An informed public is more likely to embrace the ratings and actively support political control.

Incorporating feedback mechanisms into agency operations is a useful method. Input from citizens, experts and other stakeholders is valuable for continuously improving rating systems and staying relevant. Engaging with the public ensures that agency work meets the needs and expectations of citizens.

Are the expectations eventually wrong per se, or are they just being communicated incorrectly? This must be investigated. Many conflicts arise because expectations were not clearly stated. Rather, they are merely hinted at or assumed without the other side being aware of them. To avoid misunderstandings, expectations must be communicated explicitly as a goal. If the processes are transparent, unrealistic expectations cannot arise. Everyone involved will then be informed.

By shedding light on the inner workings of government and holding leaders accountable for their actions, political rating agencies help identify areas for improvement, highlight instances of corruption or inefficiency and promote more responsible decision-making.With their tools they can contribute to transparency in politics, strengthening public trust in political institutions. At a time when democracy is facing challenges around the world, they provide a valuable opportunity to improve political culture and increase accountability. This is about how well the government is able to ensure social justice and well-being for its people.

Rating agencies keep themselves up-to-date on current developments and events, that could influence politics and its management, conducting comparative analyses, and identify parallel trends. This helps evaluate the political stability and effectiveness of government programs as well as determine the economic and social development of a country. As a side effect, transparency and accountability are promoted by making information about government performance publicly accessible.

Professional evaluations could be useful in international

politics and even for the general public to make it informed about decisions, political risks, investment opportunities and policy implications. However, there are also ethical concerns associated with political ratings, such as ensuring independence, transparency and accountability in both methods and decision-making processes. In any case, the emergence of political rating agencies reflects the increasing need for objective and reliable information in the ever-changing world of politics.

One of the United Nations' greatest deficiencies lies in one of their institutions, the Security Council, which is responsible for maintaining international peace and security. It consists of five permanent members - the United States, the United Kingdom, France, Russia and China - and has veto power over any resolution or decision. This has led to the countries mentioned using their veto rights to represent their own interests or to simply block undesirable measures. The United Nations General Assembly, in which all member states have equal representation, often lacks the power to enforce resolutions passed by the Security Council. This leads to a lack of accountability and enforces mechanisms that violate international laws and norms. The bureaucratic structures make it difficult to respond quickly to urgent crises and conflicts. In order to effectively maintain peace and justice at the global level, urgent reforms are needed. Strengthening the General Assembly and introducing new accountability mechanisms could represent first steps in the right direction to increase the UN's ability to act in a changing global landscape.

If no one is willing to take innovative responsibility at the forefront of international politics, progress will stagnate. Without strong and committed leadership important issues such as conflict resolution, climate change and global security may remain unresolved. When leaders fail to take responsibility for their actions, a culture of apathy emerges in the international community. This not only affects individual units, but the global community as a whole. How convenient it is to pass the buck and not take responsibility! It's like a game of hot potato with everyone fighting to avoid falling behind. And while policymakers play this game of political dodgeball, the rest of the world must grapple with the consequences of their inaction. It's like an endless cycle of blame that no one wants to get involved in. Let's just sit back and watch the world burn while politicians shirk any real responsibility! Who then takes responsibility?

The responsibility for political inaction and backwardness lies with those who do not commit themselves to the problems at hand. It is easy to point fingers at certain developments, but the real responsibility lies with those who choose to remain passive and uninformed. In a time when information is readily available and the consequences of ignorance are more pronounced than ever, choosing not to act is a conscious choice that perpetuates stagnation and hinders progress.

The nuclear threat remains a serious concern for the world. With approximately 13.000 nuclear weapons still in the arsenals of nine nuclear powers, the risk of a nuclear conflict is more acute than it has been in decades. Several factors exacerbate this danger: The war in Ukraine has drastically heightened tensions between Russia and the West, with Russia even hinting at the potential use of nuclear weapons. This geopolitical instability has raised alarms globally, as the specter of nuclear escalation looms larger. Moreover, nuclear disarmament efforts have stagnated worldwide. Existing arms control treaties are either being abandoned or are set to expire without renewal. New technologies, such as hypersonic weapons, further complicate the landscape, increasing uncertainty and shortening response times in crisis situations. The Treaty on the Non-Proliferation of Nuclear Weapons established in 1968, serves as the foundation for nuclear disarmament and non-proliferation. However, progress has stalled significantly and even been reversed.

The only way to mitigate this risk in the long term is through enhanced international cooperation and renewed disarmament efforts. It is imperative that nations come together to address these critical issues, fostering a safer and more secure world for future generations. The time for action is now, before the clock strikes midnight. But until then, Europe needs plausible defense elements. A german government under Angel Merkel negligently failed, in the beginning of the 21. Century, to use the protection of a common nuclear shield offered by the own neighbours. Even if the US nuclear shield remains an important part of deterrence, Europe must not become overconfident. While the western nuclear umbrella remains a critical component of Europe's security, relying too heavily on it could be risky. Changes in US political leadership or shifts in foreign policy priorities could alter the extent of US commitment to European security. Europe must therefore strive for greater strategic autonomy, developing its own capabilities to deter and respond to threats independently.

It is crucial to realistically assess the credibility and possible consequences of threats. The lessons from past administrations should serve as a wake-up call to current and future leaders: proactive measures are necessary to ensure the safety and security of the continent. Only through a comprehensive approach Europe can navigate the complexities of modern security threats and safeguard its future. This includes increasing defense spending, investing in advanced military technologies and enhancing the capabilities of European forces. The development and use of advanced technologies such as artificial intelligence, quantum computers and space-based systems are moving into the center of defense interest. Europe must ensure that its military forces are prepared to respond to a wide range of threats, from conventional military aggression to cyberattacks and hybrid warfare. This requires continuous modernization of military assets, joint exercises, and improved interoperability among European forces. Educating the public about security threats and preparedness measures is vital. A well-informed and prepared population can contribute significantly to national resilience in times of crisis.Europe must ensure that its defense capabilities are strong enough to credibly deter potential attackers. This can include both conventional and nuclear deterrents. Europes defense capabilities have to be strong enough to credibly deter potential attackers. Alliances like NATO provide collective security guarantees that can deter threats by demonstrating that an attack on one member will be treated as an attack on all.

By maintaining and potentially increasing its commitment to NATO operations, particularly in Europe, Canada can solidify its role as a key military partner. Investing in cutting-edge military technologies, such as drones, cyber defense, and artificial intelligence, Canada can contribute more effectively to joint operations and increase its strategic value as a military partner. As the Arctic becomes increasingly strategic due to climate change and shifting geopolitical interests, Canada could play a leading role in Arctic security. Collaboration with European Arctic nations like Norway and Denmark could strengthen the collective defense of this region. In addition Canada has long been a proponent of multilateralism. Participating in multilateral defense initiatives, Canada can contribute to building stronger and more resilient global security structures, from which Europe in particular benefits. Publicly demonstrating its commitment to collective defense and global security through participation in high-profile military exercises and international missions can enhance Canada's influence and credibility as a military partner. Conducting joint military exercises in the Arctic with European and NATO allies would enhance interoperability and readiness to address potential threats in the region. Canada takes also a leadership role in global non-proliferation efforts, working closely with Europe to prevent the spread of weapons of mass destruction and promote disarmament.

G. CREATIVITY IN NEW DEVELOPMENTS.

Creativity in politics is possible when political actors are open to new ideas. They just need to question existing thought patterns and then be willing to change them. Political creativity also occurs when different interest groups and actors work together and inspire each other. Furthermore, it is important that political decision-makers have the necessary resources and a clear scope to implement innovative ideas. Political creativity is possible when there is an open and dynamic political environment, that offers room for experimentation and innovation.

This openness allows for the exploration of unconventional solutions to entrenched problems, as evidenced by successful initiatives that have employed creative strategies to overcome challenges. When different interest groups and political actors come together, they can inspire one another and generate innovative ideas. This collaboration is crucial for creating a rich tapestry of perspectives that can lead to creative breakthroughs in governance. For political creativity to flourish, decision-makers must have the necessary resources and institutional support to implement innovative ideas. This includes not only financial resources but also a political climate that encourages risk-taking and experimentation, moving away from the often bureaucratic and cautious nature of government institutions. This environment must be characterized by flexibility, agility and resilience, enabling leaders to adapt to changing circumstances and embrace new opportunities for innovation. It is not just an abstract concept but a practical necessity for effective governance. It requires a commitment to openness, collaboration, resource allocation and a supportive environment that encourages innovative thinking.

By fostering these elements, political actors can drive transformative change and effectively address the complex challenges facing society today. Social creativity might best flourish, when crises produce pressure. Maybe even more so than in quiet times, when everything floats by sluggishly. Crises create immediate problems that require quick, effective solutions. This urgency can stimulate innovative thinking and break down traditional barriers to creativity. It forces to think outside the box and find new ways to utilize what is available. Crises bring together people from various backgrounds to solve common problems, leading to a cross-pollination of ideas and approaches. The current precarious situation should be used immediately on many levels.

How is creativity related to political value creation? Political communication, that is designed through creative approaches, achieves strong mobilization of the electorate. Through the use of art, visual media, storytelling and new technologies political messages are conveyed in an appealing and convincing manner. Conferences and dialog facilitate understanding and coordination between different values and perspectives. This approach emphasizes participatory virtues, pragmatic determination and moral concern in coping the challenges posed by value pluralism, particularly in collaborative fields such as environmental science.

Politics is significantly influenced by people's perceptions. Public opinion, media reporting and personal experiences shape how citizens view political issues and decisions. Politicians and political parties therefore often try to influence the public opinion and shape their messages so that they are perceived positively. In order to successfully achieve political goals, it is therefore important to understand people's perceptions and, if necessary, to influence them.

Political communication in a pluralistic society can be achieved in various ways. Pluralism is a positive response to diversity, that actively engages with differences, preserving distinct identities and beliefs. It builds a common society by respecting the inherent worth of all people and worldviews. A more rewarding approach is to simply tolerate diversity and not just insist on a single right answer.

Sociological approaches can help understand the root causes of an evil in international politics, by allowing us to analyze the underlying ideologies, interests and structures. Ethics and morals provide the guidelines to judge what is right and what is wrong. One key philosophical item is to scrutinize the ideologies, that motivate and justify unethical behavior by states and political actors. This involves critically examining nationalist or authoritarian belief systems, that dehumanize certain groups and legitimize aggression, oppression and exploitation. When governments commit acts, that violate international law, such as acts of aggression, war crimes or human rights violations, it is important that they be held accountable for their actions.

Good and evil are deeply rooted concepts that play a central role in both, personal and collective life. Stopping evil and promoting good require constant effort, reflection and commitment. While good can be held back by ignorance or institutional obstacles, fighting evil requires bold and often uncomfortable choices. Ultimately, it is the task of all humanity to seek a balance between these forces and create a world based on ethical principles, justice and compassion. This is especially true for global and international relations.

Accountability can take various forms, including legal mechanisms such as international courts or tribunals, diplomatic pressure, economic sanctions or other variants of international condemnation. By holding governments accountable for their actions, it sends a clear message that such behavior will not be tolerated and helps deter future violations of international law. This is an essential step to promote a rules-based international order and prevent impunity for serious violations of human rights and international law, which must be taken completely seriously.

Accountability is about closing gaps in the international legal order. As global interconnectedness continues to grow, the impacts of international events and issues can reverberate across the globe, affecting individuals and communities everywhere. Therefore, it is important that each and every individual, regardless of proximity to a particular event, recognizes the obligatory role in creating a more just and balanced world.

This logic can be used to evaluate the validity of

arguments and make justified judgments. Improving the international dialogue in conferences can help coordinate differences. These approaches through philosophical education help to learn how to live together in cultural diversity. They offer orientation in a diverse and often contradictory society. The open-minded dialogue is conducted through respect for different perspectives. Education continue to play the central role in individual and social development. The ability to strike a balance between awareness of the recent past and adaptability to changing circumstances is a sign of wise resilience.

Since politics is closely linked to people's perceptions, this dynamic shapes the political mainstream in several ways. Politicians adapt their policies to public opinion. Opinion polls are often used to gauge the population's attitudes. This makes it more likely that decisions, that reflect public opinion, will be implemented more consciously. The frequency and type of reporting can influence the importance the public attaches to the issues. The way the media conveys a narrative, controls the public perception. Media sometimes represents political prejudices. This steers the perception of news consumers in certain directions, leading to polarization of views.

Heated moods always have their causes. They must be classified correctly. That is the job of serious media. They have a duty to provide accurate and detailed reporting on the issues. Still, it's the heated controversies that make headlines. It seems easy to get carried away by emotions and passion. The media should strive to uncover the underlying facts. The point of criticism is the sensationalism, in which they tend to dramatize content in order to attract attention. Treating topics superficially, without sufficient analysis from outside experts, does not provide the audience with the full range of information they need to form an informed opinion.

The media's job is to uncover the underlying facts that contribute to heated debates, not judge them. One point of critics is sensationalism, where the media tends to dramatize controversial or scandalous topics, in order to attract attention and increase their press ratings. Important aspects of the content covered are often neglected or false impressions are given. The superficial treatment of headlines without sufficient background information means, that consumers do not receive all the information they need to form an informed opinion.

Sometimes the media favor certain political or social points of view and therefore report one-sidedly, as happened during the Covid pandemic or in other critical situations. Certain perspectives are underrepresented and facts are distorted. Science deniers receive a disproportionate amount of attention. A complete objectivity is not possible in practice, because journalists, like all people, have their own beliefs and prejudices. For commercial reasons it also happens that a false balance is drawn in order to generate more attention and clicks. For this reason, regular third-party assessments are absolutely necessary. Such cooperation with evaluation agencies would be an important step to strengthen the quality of reporting. Overall, new, promising opportunities are opening up in the media industry. Traditional habits are changing and at the same time new, specialized roles are emerging.

The rise of social media exacerbates the situation, as emotional content garners more attention, overshadowing critical analysis and expert insights. Emotionally charged contributions overshadow nuanced discussions, that require careful analysis and understanding of international relations. Important topics like trade agreements, military interventions or climate change negotiations may be oversimplified, making it difficult for the public to grasp the complexities involved.

The heightened emotional response has negative consequences, such as spreading hatred or outrage. Such negative emotions are often driven by platforms' algorithms. Misinformation spread rapidly, when it is framed in an emotionally appealing way. This leads to widespread misconceptions about international events, policies or actors, complicating public understanding and discourse. There are also users, who want to engage with content, rather than with headlines that reinforce their existing beliefs. What is happening at the moment is, that echo chambers are formed, that limit access to alternative perspectives. This is hindering any constructive dialogue and compromise in international relations. Misinformation can spread quickly, if it is phrased in an emotionally appealing way. This leads to widespread misunderstandings about international events, policies or actors, making public understanding and useful discourse difficult.

By sharing best practices and creating common guidelines, the EU can help spread global awareness of the risks of emotional manipulation on social media. Promoting innovation in media literacy and the development of technologies, that detect and prevent emotional manipulation, the EU could take a proactive approach. Professional social media platforms can facilitate discussions, that bring together diverse voices and enable the exchange of ideas and perspectives, that might otherwise be overlooked. However, they should ensure that transparency information is not only available, but also understandable for the "average user".

While social media platforms have their challenges, such as the risk of echo chambers and misinformation, they also offer significant opportunities to facilitate meaningful discussions involving diverse voices. By promoting inclusivity with interactivity and providing access to a wide range of perspectives, these platforms can play a critical role in enriching public discourse and advancing understanding in an increasingly connected world.

Irrational influencers can pose various dangers, particularly with regard to the spread of fake news, extremist views and problematic content. These dangers can affect the way their followers form their opinions. Influencers often mix facts and opinions, leading to the spread of disinformation. Influencers from extremist or racist spectrums use social media to expand their reach and spread dangerous ideologies.

The algorithmically controlled "For You" feed often displays videos on potentially harmful topics, which is particularly problematic for very young users. How Tiktok influences the planning of „Generation Z" through supposed insider tips, for example by influencing the consumption of various products. If certain topics are promoted, it could lead to mental health problems such as depression or anxiety, and the red card should be shown. It becomes particularly critical for voters in the area of international relations, if TikTok not only collects data, but also censors content. This inevitably leads to a distortion of public discourse and affects the perception of certain topics. The threats posed by Tiktok also matters Europe.

To understand how populism, propaganda and misinformation are spread nowadays and why racial parties are successful on TikTok, it is important to recognize the strategies used. Success comes from the ability to use the platform effectively and present an image that resonates with specific audiences. Unlike other movements, the radical approach is characterized by an inherent nationalism and racism that affects a significant part of users. By focusing on a simplistic narrative, radical parties have managed to gain a significant following, as evidenced by their millions of likes on the platform.

Since politicians use various techniques to influence public opinion, including rhetoric, advertising and public appearances, they can also use professional platforms of rating agencies to use logical arguments and ethical considerations to persuade their target groups. Social media has become a powerful tool for political messaging. It allows for direct communication with the public and the rapid dissemination of information. However, it also presents challenges, such as the spread of misinformation and echo chambers. Clear and consistent messaging helps building trust and credibility.

Destructive elements can generally be defeated. This statement honors the philosophical belief that good can ultimately triumph over evil, but also emphasizes the practical and political implications of this idea. History has indeed shown that societies and governments have been able to defeat destructive forces through resilience, unity, and perseverance. By continuously working to address the root causes of extremism, promoting dialogue and understanding and implementing effective security measures, progress can be made in countering threats to peace and stability. The fight against destructive elements is an ongoing battle that requires sustained commitment and vigilance from individuals, communities and governments. It is not an easy task, and it requires possibly years of sustained effort. It's essential to maintain a strong commitment to the cause, even in the face of setbacks or challenges. Perseverance and determination are particularly important in the fight against destructive elements.

The global community has been closely following the events unfolding in Ukraine, particularly in the aftermath of the Russian invasion. The situation has sparked widespread concern and condemnation from world leaders, international organizations and civil society due to the grave violations of international law and human rights, that have been reported. The initial days of the invasion were marked by shocking acts of violence and brutality, including reports of indiscriminate attacks on civilians, arbitrary detentions, torture and extrajudicial killings by Russian mercenary troops. These actions have been widely documented through eyewitness accounts, videos, and other evidence, leading to calls for accountability and justice from the international community. Despite the overwhelming evidence and outcry from various quarters, there are challenges in ensuring that the world pays attention to and addresses the atrocities committed in Ukraine.

Factors such as disinformation, geopolitical interests and the complexity of the conflict may contribute to a lack of widespread awareness and understanding in some parts of the world. It will be necessary to choose between freedom and terror. It is easy to overlook the fact that, what would ultimately harm Ukraine, would cause severe pain to the lungs of Eastern Europe as a whole. How are explosive areas calmed down? After a conflict, building stable and effective institutions is essential. This includes establishing the rule of law, promoting human rights and establishing a transparent political system with comprehensive economic support, especially from outside.

However, if dialogue proves insufficient to resolve conflict, additional strategies and approaches need to be established. By using external competent mediators, gaps between the conflict parties can be closed. They must offer perspectives, suggest creative solutions and facilitate communication. Effective facilitation in international relations requires a combination of strategies and intense commitment. Conversely, targeted sanctions and pressure can be used to force the parties to return to negotiations or comply with agreements. Sanctions must be carefully designed to avoid harm to the civilian population as much as possible. Ensuring that there is a plan for post-conflict reconstruction and long-term peacebuilding is a condition sine qua non for all efforts.

The models available are aimed at politicians who, from their perspective, would like support as a feedback from the civil society. Who is civil society? To put it simply, it is all of us, individuals and groups from different areas of business, research, sport, crafts and service providers or culture. They are forming networks in intellectual forums and common venues. Civil society includes everyone who participates in the social structure outside of state and corporate structures. It is these diverse voices, that resonate with the needs and desires of the broader community.

They draw parallels between different facts or situations, in order to identify commonalities or similarities to establish a connection between them. They gain new insights and develop solutions according to the specifications. Parallels can be drawn in many everyday situations, they only have to be based on well-founded information and factual arguments and not drawn arbitrarily. If the EU wants to ensure a strong economic and social order, the social market economy must not only guarantee the prosperity of its citizens, but also create a stable and fair environment in many places both internally and externally. This balance between economic freedom and social security is at the heart of a European model, that adapts competition policy to globalization. This means that Europe remains competitive on a global scale.

The structures of the European Union could play a pioneering role in this process, as they already bring together a wide range of political actors and interest groups, creating a complex political space, that goes beyond traditional party lines. There already exist forms of cooperation and coalitions that are not based on party affiliation. It is entirely possible that traditional party formations will become less important in the future and that other idea-based coalitions will prevail instead. This could be done through a greater focus on individual policy issues or ideas rather than entire party programs. This is what party apparatchiks fear most.

The nostalgia for past structures leads to the depressing sphere of labeling long-outdated framework conditions. Parties that adhere to them have difficulty adapting to new political, social and technological developments. This affects their ability to respond effectively to current challenges. If parties do not keep up with the times and modernize their structures and strategies, they risk becoming unattractive to voters, especially to the younger generations. Parties anchored in the past, often show strong resistance to change, which limits their ability to adapt to new political realities. If the structures do not evolve, political parties will fall behind in competition with more agile and modern political movements. Parties that adhere to outdated ideologies have difficulty forming coalitions with more modern or progressive groups limiting their political influence.

For example, while left-wing parties in history often benefited from the spread of misinformation, conservative parties were known for misinterpretation. However, both must recognize that these days are over. It's almost as if democracy is in an ironic competition to see which side has eroded public trust more quickly. Who needs trust in political institutions when you can have cynicism instead? The idea that parties are based on poor bureaucracy could undermine trust in the entire political system - everywhere. But what good is a democracy, if there is populism and polarization? It can lead to a breakdown in civil discourse, making it difficult to reach consensus. When political opponents are seen as enemies rather than rivals, the spirit of cooperation essential to democracy is eroded. This results in majoritarianism, where the majority's will is imposed without regard for minority rights, weakening the inclusiveness that is fundamental to democracy. It becomes difficult to pass laws or implement policies when consensus is seen as betrayal by both sides. It is the cause of gridlock and ineffective governance. People become so disillusioned with the democratic process that they are willing to support authoritarian measures or leaders, believing that only a strong hand can resolve societal divisions. Despite these challenges, democracy also has mechanisms for self-correction. The presence of free elections, an independent judiciary, and a vibrant civil society can counterbalance the negative effects of populism and polarization. Despite these negative experiences, democracy also has mechanisms for self-correction. The presence of free elections, an independent judiciary and a vibrant civil society can offset the effects of populism and polarization. An informed and engaged electorate is essential in holding leaders accountable and ensuring that democratic norms are upheld, even in the face of populist rhetoric or polarized politics. It simply needs to be given the opportunity to obtain information and to receive objective, knowledge-based assessments and evaluations from rating agencies. A healthy democracy requires constant vigilance, adaptation and commitment to its foundational principles, especially in times of political and social stress.

In an era of widespread misinformation and "fake news," the media plays a critical role in fact-checking claims made by different sides. After all, they are the heroes of the drama, tirelessly exposing wrongdoing and informing the public – at least in an ideal world. In reality, we depend on sensational headlines and biased reporting. An active civil society? That's almost like saying unicorns exist. Of course, public debates can put pressure on political parties, to demand change. But who has the energy for such committed behavior today? The classic party system could actually be outdated. By modeling respectful and fact-based discourse, the media can help reduce polarization. This involves not only how journalists report but also how they moderate discussions among political leaders, experts, and the public. It can be a force for good, promoting accountability and informed public discourse, but it can also contribute to division and misinformation, if not handled responsibly.

Reimagining Europe means dismantling nationalism and traditional party constructs, a concept that may sound idealistic but is becoming increasingly necessary in today's fragmented political situations. Nationalism, which for a short period of time in history served to unite small, fragmented regions into cohesive nation-states, now often acts as a barrier to broader integration. It promotes division rather than unity and creates an environment, in which citizens see themselves as separate rather than part of a larger European community. Appreciating Europe's diverse cultures strengthens its citizens' sense of solidarity.

Harmonizing economic policies across Europe can reduce differences between his members and lead to greater stability and prosperity for all Europeans. Implementing pan-European social programs can ensure a safety net for all citizens, reduce inequality and stabilize a sense of shared responsibility. Education and political awareness are the key to moving forward. But why bother encouraging critical thinking when it's so much easier to be entertained by the next viral fake news story?

Smart growth, to be called intelligent, means investing in research and development to promote innovation and generate new knowledge. This requires expanding education and lifelong learning to optimize people's capabilities. Incentives to invest in new technologies and digital solutions are the prerequisite for sustainable growth. If resource efficiency and the circular economy are promoted, the framework conditions for fair income distribution and social security must be created at the same time.

In modern times, when traditional party structures seem outdated and unresponsive, shifting attention to more dynamic forms of political engagement may be the answer. The introduction of alternative tools would create a more inclusive and responsive policy environment. Education and political awareness remain fundamental to this change, as a well-informed population is better equipped to engage in meaningful discourse. However, critical thinking and political competence require effort and investment from all sides in the willingness to engage with what is happening in current events.

The best possible future for Europe depends on how credible, competent and efficient the EU institutions are. Within the larger units themselves, flexible and performance-oriented movements are emerging instead to closely aligned parties. With the pioneering spirit, Europe's reputation appears more appealing and stable. The isolated attempts of nationalism should not spread to all of Europe. European politics is therefore working on the appropriate adjustments. Similar to sports training, the details are shaped without losing sight of the big picture.

New developed adminsitrative large-scale units can respond more efficiently to common challenges and exploit synergies between neighboring areas. They can develop common infrastructure, research facilities and educational programs that go beyond current national borders. Political parties, as we know them from yesterday, can give rise to interest movements, that respond more flexibly and dynamically to the needs of tomorrow. Such structures are not bound by rigid party shackles and ideologies. They could can band together around specific issues or concerns like environmental issues, social justice or digital innovation, enabling more targeted and effective policymaking.

We can expect that changing interest groups will always be in flux and influence policy direction. The ability to effectively manage this flexibility will be critical to successful policy outcomes. Interest groups evolve and change over time due to changing societal needs, economic conditions and cultural trends. In order not to lose touch, political decision-makers must act quickly. A balance must be found that satisfies the various interest groups while achieving the policy goals set. To successfully navigate the boat of wavering interest groups, policymakers must be able to practice political management appropriately.

The determining themes for new political structures are above all ethical principles such as freedom, security and justice. They are immediately followed by the performance principle in business and research under the ecological premise of protecting the environment and nature. These principles serve as a basis for building effective European governance. The focus is on efficiency, effectiveness and accountability. The potential advantages of structural change can only be exploited if cooperation in the planning and implementation process is guaranteed. Constant professional observation, evaluation and analysis make it possible to draw optimal conclusions for implementation.

Outside Europe, a similar political model of large regions could be considered as an alternative to the two-state solution in the Middle East conflict. This approach focuses on creating a larger framework for regional cooperation and integration in the Middle East. Since the conflict is based on long-standing historical and religious claims, a two-state system will not be sufficient to resolve the existing differences. The ongoing violence and instability in the region illustrate, that a two-state project is not relevant to a solution. Regular outbreaks of violence, such as in Gaza, show the fragility of all temporary agreements.

Compromises lead to a superficial view of the problem, that does not cover the core issue. For example, temporary ceasefires reduce immediate tensions, but the underlying grievances and expectations are not addressed, leaving the door wide open for future wars. Key issues related to sovereignty, borders, refugee status and security arrangements remain unresolved in the two-state system. This creates ongoing uncertainty and mistrust and makes it difficult to envision lasting peace. Given these challenges, finding alternative solutions that include a broader regional approach is a possible way forward.

Priority is given to international efforts to isolate the terrorist formations that are operating. Such programs include also topics such as the right of return for refugees, territorial integration and the status of Jerusalem. In matters of Israeli settlement policy, which primarily emphasizes nationalist intentions, a multi-regional solution would be recommended too. The deep-rooted hostilities, which will certainly continue for some time, can only be gradually leveled off with comprehensive and sophisticated programs.

Macro-regional constructs provide an opportunity to combat terrorism when multiple countries pool resources, information and strategies. A common intelligence network enables the efficient exchange of information, which illuminates the identification of terrorist cells and the tracking of their activities. The merged states would form joint task forces capable of responding quickly and precisely in crisis situations. A large regional project would contribute to the de-radicalization and prevention of extremist ideologies through social and educational programs.

A multilateral peace agreement between Israel, Palestine, Jordan, Lebanon, Syria and other regional actors would have to address the core problems of the conflicts. Promoting economic integration could benefit all participating countries through shared infrastructure projects, trade and economic development. A macro-regional approach would also promote the joint management of critical resources such as water and energy. This creates mutual dependencies that increase the incentives for peace. By introducing new models, it would be possible to create a more stable and prosperous environment for all residents. Middle Eastern countries have abundant renewable energy resources, particularly solar and wind energy. Europe could seek massive participation.

While negotiations during war certainly face obstacles, framing them as a "necessary evil" overlooks their potential constructive role. When conducted in good faith, negotiations can be a valuable tool for conflict management, de-escalation, and eventually resolving the underlying disputes that led to war. Their utility goes beyond simply managing power relations to potentially saving lives and creating pathways to peace. International negotiations are viewed as a dynamic, iterative process that requires continuous learning and adaptation. But what would international politics be without missteps? A negotiating table can quickly become the setting for a political soap opera, where national interests collide with personal egos and every gesture and word is scrutinized. Does it entertain the viewer as world leaders plan their next moves and behave like chess players in a game of intrigue, like in a poorly written thriller?

If we turn to political communication in general, not only in war situations but also in daily exchanges of information or in common political disputes, we find that misunderstandings occur very often. They have different causes, especially from different backgrounds. Assumptions based on stereotypes or previous experiences easily lead to misinterpretations. Stress and anxiety impair the ability to share interests effectively. The use of vague language also attracts different interpretations. Without understanding the language, one will not understand the political question.

Cultures also differ in their indirect time orientation. Polychronic cultures, such as Latin America or the Middle East, view time as flexible, with multitasking becoming common. Monochronic cultures, such as North America and Europe, tend to view time as linear with strict schedules. Polychronic cultures may be more comfortable with ambiguous deadlines and changing priorities. Consensus-based decision making is easier in cultures like Japan, where decisions are made collectively by unanimous agreement. In contrast, top-down decision making is more prevalent in cultures such as the United States, where decisions are made by individuals, often managers, judges or executives, and are less influenced by others. When collaborating across cultures, it will always be important to align with the expectations of the opposite.

To make meaningful progress on global problems, developing comprehensive and multi-faceted solutions is essential. The aim is to take a systemic approach, introduce multilateral coordination and integrate different perspectives and expertise. Systems thinking means connecting the different components within a system and recognizing how changes in one part can affect the whole. What the change brings must be clarified in advance, otherwise everything will sink into the swamp of contradictions. What problem is the change intended to solve? What are the specific goals and objectives? Setting a clear goal helps ensure the change process and its direction. Possible after-effects and unintended consequences need to be examined, as do long-term strategies, that deal with future impacts.

Integrating diverse perspectives and expertise ensures that solutions are comprehensive and all aspects of a problem have been considered. This promotes innovation and co-creation. Inclusive participation involves involving a wide range of stakeholders in the decision-making process, including governments, the private sector, academia and civil society. Involving local communities in the development and implementation of solutions ensures that they are contextually appropriate and socially acceptable. Intercultural competence within teams helps to effectively manage and utilize cultural differences. Adaptive management strategies allow for flexibility and adjustment of policies and actions based on new information and constantly changing circumstances. Fostering a culture of continuous learning and improvement encourages both feedback and iteration to refine solutions over time.

Professional scenario planning, such as that carried out in think tanks or evaluation agencies, is particularly valuable because it enables the anticipation of various future states of the system and the development of strategies that must be robust under a wide variety of conditions. Interdisciplinary collaboration is essential as it integrates different disciplines to gain a comprehensive understanding of the problem.

Let's take a look at the supposed beauty of echo chambers. "Who needs different perspectives and a broad consensus when tunnel vision is so reassuring? And innovation? Why bother with new ideas when your own views are completely reliable? Silos are the fortress that protects and ensures the chaos of creativity that innovation gathers dust where it actually belongs. Why involve the annoying communities affected? It is much more efficient to ignore them completely and be surprised when the isolated statements fall to the ground with a loud thud. It's a small price to pay for our loneliness. Who has the time to understand different perspectives when entertaining anecdotes arise from misunderstandings? Overrated rigidity in sticking to solutions that are set in stone. Changed circumstances? They are just an opportunity to showcase one's own inflexibility." This ironic depiction highlights the absurdity of ignoring inclusiveness, fresh ideas, social engagement, cultural understanding and adaptability in decision-making processes.

The European Union has always been a pioneer when it comes to setting ambitious goals. However, aiming high is one thing, reaching the goals is another.To turn its vision into reality, the EU needs a rebalance of the existing institutions. Some may require restructuring to better adapt to new priorities, while others may need to be rebuilt from the ground up to address the specific challenges. This requires the necessary reduction of nationalism and the reorientation of membership in the European Council, away from nation states towards a few regional members as well as the dismantling of traditional party systems.

The EU therefore has the opportunity to develop new

dynamics through increased regional cooperation and a focus on pan-European challenges. Instead of getting lost in national egoism, closer cooperation between regions could pave the way to a sustainable EU. Cross-national initiatives offer enormous potential for tackling common problems and learning from each other. Whether infrastructure, environmental protection or economic development - in many areas better solutions can be found by pooling resources and knowledge than going it alone. The EU already promotes such cooperation through programs such as „Interreg", which enable concrete projects to further develop the regions. At the same time, strengthening pan-European political movements could bring a breath of fresh air to EU institutions that are often perceived as distant from citizens. If more people across national borders get involved in European issues, this can lead to a change in mentality and bring the EU closer to its citizens. In order to remain globally competitive, Europe must also join forces in key areas. Strengthening the common foreign and security policy is necessary to meet the challenges of an increasingly complex global landscape. Given the current crisis situation, this is not a fairy tale.

Massive investments in future technologies such as artificial intelligence, quantum computing and biotechnology are necessary in order not to lose out in the global innovation race. Building a competitive digital economy and targeted support for cutting-edge research and start-ups can make Europe an innovation initiator. At the same time, it is important to drive change towards a sustainable economy and society. With the European Green Deal, the EU has set itself ambitious goals. These require profound changes in all areas - from energy supply and mobility to production and consumption patterns. It must be ensured that the transition is socially fair and that existing inequalities are reduced. Promoting the circular economy and sustainable mobility concepts are further important building blocks on the path to a sustainable Europe. Getting there requires the courage to change and the willingness to think and act across national borders. But the opportunities that arise are worth taking on these challenges.

The first step to strengthening the EU would be to find out what its top priorities are. This is not just about unmasking bureaucracies, but also about ensuring that the existing structures are flexible enough to respond adequately to changing needs. Once the priorities are set, the next step is to ensure that there are enough resources to achieve the goals. This means dealing with the necessary financial, human and material resources. Beyond that, it's about mobilizing expertise and ensuring the right people are in the right places to drive these plans forward. When trying to combine the best elements, it must be ensured they work together harmoniously. Otherwise, a big dream will quickly turn into an amusing mess - and the audience may end up talking more about the funny misadventures than the attractions themselves!

First and foremost, European citizens have a legitimate interest in how European trade, security and climate policies directly impact their daily lives. EU decisions on trade agreements have an impact on labor markets, consumer prices and economic stability. No less important is the impact of Europe's stance on environmental issues on public health and the quality of life of its citizens. The various partners outside the geographical borders of the continent may also ask themselves how Europe sees them, and conversely, Europe will assess how the others outside are doing. How could European democracy ideally work? And then, there is the assessment of citizens in the event of armed conflict. How affected do they feel?

There is no country or confederation in the world quite like the European Union, when it comes to its unique governance structure and democratic processes. The EU's system is characterized by the interplay between management, parliamentary decision-making and leadership that creates a distinctive triangular relationship of democratic influence. The task of the European Parliament is not to plunge unprepared into the uncertainty about the future of Europe. The topics are prepared by an independent institution, the European Commission. However, as soon as the political environment is dominated by irrational emotions such as nationalism or decision-selfishness, political activities spiral out of control. The economic and social damage affects the unity. So it is important that the focus is on regions and countries and not on nations. Then parts of a country are even grouped into different large regions, so that the functional division benefits the entire country. The economic potential and social justice as well as the control over defense are at the center of considerations for joint decisions.

The task of the European Parliament is not to plunge unprepared into the uncertainty about the future of Europe. The topics are prepared by an independent institution, the European Commission. As soon as the political environment is dominated by irrational emotions such as nationalism or selfishness, political activities spiral out of control. The economic and social damage affects unity. Therefore, it is important that the focus is on regions and countries and not on nations. Then parts of a country are even grouped into different large regions so that the functional division benefits the entire country. Economic potential and social justice as well as control over weapons systems are at the center of considerations for joint decisions.

The Parliament has to ensure informed and evidence-based debates. This requires access to high-quality data, research results and expert opinions. Building stronger links with academic institutions and think tanks can enrich the parliamentary discussions. Ensuring that all voices of all regions are heard is crucial to democratic legitimacy. The Parliament should promote inclusive dialogue and create platforms for the different perspectives. Involving the public in parliamentary debates increases transparency and accountability.

The management of the European Commission must be robust and equipped with streamlined processes and a results-oriented focus. Investing in modern management practices can significantly increase efficiency. To effectively address the critical issues facing European policies, the Commission needs to improve its management capacity in several key areas, as it needs to develop comprehensive rapid response and recovery strategies to ensure that the EU is better prepared for future crises. Introducing rigorous evaluation mechanisms and promoting a culture of openness will help curb corruption and inefficiency in European fields. By focusing on these areas, the European Commission increases its effectiveness and responsiveness, ultimately leading to more resilient governance structures within the EU.

The European Council is a cornerstone of the EU's decision-making process, providing strategic direction and facilitating cooperation amongts members. The conclusions drawn from these meetings guide the work of the European Commission and other EU institutions. During times of crisis, whether economic, political, or social, the European Council convenes to formulate a coordinated response. For example, during the Eurozone crisis, it played a pivotal role in agreeing on financial assistance packages and reforms.The Council fosters cooperation among its members, encouraging consensus-building to align the member's positions on common challenges. Implementing clear metrics for evaluating the effectiveness of policies and programs can improve the accountability. Regular audits and assessments can identify areas of inefficiency and corruption, ensuring that resources are used effectively. Incorporating sustainability into all aspects of policy-making can ensure that the EU not only addresses immediate challenges but also builds long-term resilience against future crises.

The EU is still facing significant challenges that stem from inadequate organizational frameworks. To counteract these disintegrating forces, it is crucial for the EU to continuously improve its structures and processes while enhancing collaboration and trust among the different countries. Only by doing so can the EU function as a stable and united community, effectively addressing the complex issues it encounters. A reasonable analysis of problems and challenges is necessary to make informed decisions and bring about positive changes. While uniting political forces leads to common goals and solutions, the diversity of opinions and ideas should not be neglected. It is important to respect different political currents and viewpoints and to recognize and combat extremist tendencies in a timely manner. Through dialogue, collaboration and respectful exchange, political actors can find constructive solutions and promote political creativity without being overwhelmed by extremist developments..

The European unity is still confronted with significant internal threats arising from inadequate organizational framework conditions. To counteract these disintegrating forces, it is crucial for the EU to continually improve its structures and processes while strengthening cooperation and trust between different countries and regions. Only in this way can the EU function as a stable and united community and effectively address the complex problems it faces. An in-depth analysis of the issues is necessary to make informed decisions and bring about positive change. While united political forces can lead to common goals and solutions, the diversity of opinions and ideas should not be neglected. It is important to respect different political currents and viewpoints, but at the same time to recognize and combat extremist tendencies that take place outside the democratic framework. Through collaboration and respectful exchange of ideas, political actors can find constructive solutions and promote political creativity without being overwhelmed by extremist developments.

Optimal co-creation requires open and transparent communication between everyone involved. This means that information and data must be freely exchanged to create a common knowledge base. By using digital platforms and tools, governments and organizations can facilitate collaboration and information sharing. If an announced trend reversal is not used, there will be massive negative consequences, because without the necessary changes being implemented, problems will continue to exist or even worsen. This only aggreviates the international situation and thus the quality of life of many people.

One of the most damaging reactions to the unpredictability of modern life is to react with panic and excitement. When faced with uncertainty, people's natural tendency might be to react impulsively, which often increases the feeling of disorder rather than alleviating it. This creates a vicious cycle of fear and misinterpretation that only increases personal and community distress. However, those who strive to understand the larger picture and the underlying dynamics of events can maintain their composure even in the most turbulent times. By identifying patterns and contextualizing separate events within the larger context, individuals can move through crises with a more balanced and informed perspective.

It is also important for the general public, i.e. for all citizens, to keep an eye on the big lines. Anyone who deals with the connections will maintain personal calm even in the turbulence of the world. The worst reaction is to scream and lash out as a troublemaker. Focusing on overarching trends and broader contexts, rather than getting bogged down in minutiae, helps reduce excessive anxiety and avoid poor judgment. This perspective is not only beneficial, but essential to maintaining a sense of personal calm in the midst of global upheaval.

The key to achieving this level of knowledge is continuous learning and expanding consciousness. Using reliable sources of information, engaging in serious discussions and reviewing historical precedents lead to a more comprehensive view of current events. This approach helps distinguish between immediate, temporary problems and those that are of lasting importance. Additionally, practicing patience and resilience is essential. Quick and superficial solutions may provide temporary relief, but often do not address the root causes of stress and confusion. Instead, a calm, measured approach allows for more effective problem-solving and decision-making.

It's really good to know what just seems threatening and what is downright threatening and what isn't. Distinguishing between perceived threats and actual dangers is important for making informed decisions. Experts must evaluate the source of information and the conclusions. Sometimes there are situations that appear dangerous, due to limited information, stereotypes or misinformation. They cause emotional reactions, such as fear or anxiety. Hazards that pose a concrete risk to safety can be proven through evidence and analysis. Real threats require action to mitigate potential damage. Misguided policies can lead to overregulation, civil liberties violations, or inadequate responses to real risks. To create effective interventions, decisions must be made based on accurate threat assessments. In international relations misinterpreted threats are often due to misinterpretations, propaganda or political hostilities. Media, political rhetoric or cultural misunderstandings reinforce the misconceptions. Clear communication and shared intelligence support factual disclosure.

In a time characterized by tension and conflict, moments of pause are more important than ever. These moments should therefore be actively used and promoted to rethink sustainable and peaceful coexistence. Co-creation in international politics can be defined as a process in which governments, international organizations, non-governmental organizations, civil society and other stakeholders work together to develop and implement policy solutions. This approach is based on the idea that the participation of different actors with different perspectives and competencies leads to better and more sustainable results.

What do we expect from modern international politics and its actors? Political leaders must stay abreast of new trends, technologies and societal changes. This will be achieved through regular collaboration with experts, scientists and innovators. Leaders should actively seek insights from diverse areas to understand new developments and integrate them into policy making. Policies should be implemented with built-in mechanisms for collecting feedback from the public and different stakeholders. Assessments inform ongoing adjustments and improvements to ensure policies remain relevant and effective. Policies must be adaptable and allow for changes as circumstances change and new information emerges. Flexibility ensures that policy evolves to meet the current and future needs of society.

For an inclusive dialogue with civil society, it will be necessary to involve a wide range of stakeholders. Different perspectives help to understand the complexity of problems and to find holistic solutions. Proactive policymaking means anticipating future challenges as best as possible. Rapid and effective responses are critical to maintaining public trust and ensuring stability. A satisfactory future in international politics requires a departure from traditional power dynamics and the development of new ideas for global order. As the world becomes more interconnected, international cooperation and multilateral institutions will be key to addressing common challenges.

However, Europe in particular is struggling to develop a coherent strategic vision and lacks the military capabilities to be a major player on the world stage.

Overcoming this requires deeper integration and a willingness to extend sovereignty for the common good. At the same time, the proliferation of weapons of mass destruction and the rise of irresponsible actors mean that the deterrence logic of the Cold War no longer clearly applies. Preventing the use of these weapons and addressing regional conflicts will be critical priorities. Ultimately, creating a satisfactory international order in the 21st century requires creative thinking, courageous leadership and a commitment to diplomacy and the peaceful resolution of disputes. It won't be easy, but the alternative – a world of unilateralism, great power competition and the constant threat of conflict – is unacceptable. The future may be uncertain, but it is up to us to shape it. Europe's responsibility in the global community underlines its role in addressing global challenges. Europe cannot avoid its contribution to international cooperation, sustainability and development efforts.

In economy, threats can arise from a variety of sources, including global market fluctuations, geopolitical tensions and changes in consumer behavior. When governments perceive these threats, they may take protectionist measures that can affect global trade and economic stability. However, a nuanced understanding of real economic threats helps countries implement measures to protect their economies without resorting to unnecessary trade barriers. Sudden changes in commodity prices, currency fluctuations or stock market instability pose risks to economies. By establishing trade relationships with a wider range of countries, countries reduce their vulnerability to economic shocks.

When economic situations are shaken by ideological imperatives, such as those prevalent in Communist China, survival strategies in international relations can change significantly. Ideological decisions that deviate from economic rationality can lead to uncertainty and instability, particularly at key junctures in global trade and diplomacy. This could happen, for example, by strengthening regional alliances or realigning trade relations. Hotspots such as strategically important trade routes or regions with significant natural resources could be a particular focus.

In addition, geopolitical alliances could shift as countries seek to protect their interests and protect themselves from negative impacts. Countries may be forced to seek alternative partners or reduce their economic dependence. At the same time, China may seek to consolidate its power and influence through bilateral agreements or by promoting regional trading blocs. Economic policy ideologies that deviate from the prevailing paradigms challenge the established economic and political orders. This can lead to conflicts between states with different economic policy orientations and make international cooperation more difficult

Radical economic policy experiments can lead to increased volatility on the global markets and shake investor confidence.

The modern economy has indeed evolved to embrace compliance rules across all industries and sectors, reflecting a significant shift from past practices. This transformation is driven by several factors and has far-reaching implications for businesses, governments, and the global economic structure. Compliance has transformed from a passive, reactive approach to a proactive one that leverages advanced technologies and data analytics. This evolution has been particularly notable over the past five decades, with compliance programs becoming increasingly sophisticated and integral to business operations. This approach allows companies to identify patterns, manage risks more effectively, and respond swiftly to emerging compliance issues. However, it's crucial to note that while data analytics is a powerful tool, it does not replace a well-integrated compliance program.

Today's compliance frameworks extend beyond mere legal adherence. They now encompass environmental, social responsibility consideration and societal benefits.This expanded scope reflects a growing recognition that a company's impact extends far beyond its financial performance. The unethical practices that unscrupulous tycoons once employed - exploiting technological advantages for personal gain due to a lack of oversight - would now have the potential to destabilize the entire global economic structure. Today, only intelligent and ethical management methods can deliver sustainable value. To ensure that the era of economic arbitrariness remains a thing of the past, international regulations must be respected. Global politics is also governed by these rules and is dependent on their enforcement. By ensuring that businesses operate within established regulatory boundaries, these rules contribute to overall economic stability.

The EU is known for its comprehensive regulatory framework that spans a wide range of industries, including finance, data protection, environmental standards, and consumer rights. By establishing these regulations, the EU aims to ensure a level playing field, promote fair competition, and protect the interests of consumers and businesses alike. This directly supports the idea that only intelligent and ethical management practices, within a regulated environment, can create sustainable value.

The EU internal market is based on the harmonization of standards in its member states. This means that products and services must meet uniform standards across the EU to ensure that companies operate under the same rules regardless of the country in which they are based. This is a practical implementation of the idea that global or regional rules must be respected to prevent economic arbitrariness and ensure stability.

The EU's regulatory standards often have a global impact, as companies around the world must comply with EU regulations if they wish to do business within the EU. This extends the EU's influence beyond its borders and reinforces the importance of international politics and cooperation in maintaining economic stability and fairness.

Supporting research at an international level helps industry adapt to technological changes and remain competitive. Instead of imposing tariffs, governments can support struggling industries through grants, training programs and infrastructure investments. Participation in well-calculated international trade agreements creates a more stable trading environment and reduces the likelihood of unilateral protectionism. However, it must also be recognized that conflicts may lead to sanctions or trade restrictions that affect economic relations. Rapid advances in technology are making certain industries obsolete, leading to job losses and economic changes.

The EU has positioned itself as a leader in climate action and has significantly influenced international climate policies, particularly through its commitment to the Paris Agreement and its ambitious climate goals setting benchmarks for other countries. Many countries and international organizations view the EU's climate leadership positively, appreciating its proactive stance and ambitious targets. The Green Deal and its commitment to decarbonization and sustainability have been lauded as comprehensive and forward-thinking initiatives. For instance, the regulatory frameworks and carbon pricing mechanisms are frequently cited as models for other regions. The EU provides financial and technological support to developing countries to help them achieve their climate goals. This support is generally well-received and contributes to the EU's positive international reputation.

However, by some trading partners the EU's use of carbon border adjustment measures to regulate imports from countries with lower environmental standards is viewed as protectionist. Developing countries sometimes perceive the EU's climate policies as imposing unfair burdens on them, especially if they lack the resources to meet similar standards. The principle of common but differentiated responsibilities is crucial in this context. In authoritarian regimes, a lack of transparency and restrictions on civil society can make it difficult to implement environmental and climate policies. Conspiracy ideologies targeting the Green Deal and the liberal world order have proliferated, reflecting deeper anxieties and resistance within various segments of society. These ideologies often stem from a complex interplay of factors, including economic concerns and political disillusionment. Nevertheless, the Green Deal possesses significant potential to stimulate economic competition. By driving innovation, encouraging technological advancements and reshaping market dynamics, the Green Deal a more competitive and dynamic economic environment can be promoted.

It stimulates significant investments in renewable energy, energy efficiency and sustainable technologies. The increased funding offers companies the opportunity to innovate and develop cutting-edge technologies in sectors such as solar energy and wind power. Companies and research institutions are motivated to explore new solutions that lead to breakthroughs that improve competitiveness. Sectors such as sustainable agriculture, green building and waste management are expected to grow, providing companies with new opportunities for investment and expansion. Companies that excel in these technologies can enter international markets, increasing their competitiveness on a global scale. The small agricultural structures that produce naturally are enhanced. Companies that adopt circular economy principles and sustainable practices can reduce their costs and improve their market position. Lower energy costs and less reliance on fossil fuels increase operational efficiency and give companies a competitive advantage.

So the „Green Deal" is more than an environmental policy; it is a catalyst for economic competition. By driving innovation, creating new market opportunities, enhancing industry efficiency, attracting investment and encouraging sustainable practices, it has the potential to transform the economic landscape. As businesses and countries adapt to these changes, they will compete to lead in the new economy, fostering a dynamic and competitive environment that benefits both the economy and the environment.

The discrepancy between humanitarian responsibilities and geopolitical interests is evident in Europe's response to various crises. While there are some cases where humanitarian assistance is provided on a large scale - such as natural disasters or certain conflicts - there are also situations where the response is slow or inadequate, often due to political considerations or internal tensions within the EU. As part of the international community, Europe not only has the responsibility to respond to humanitarian crises, but also to act preventatively. This means addressing the causes of conflict and suffering, not just treating the symptoms. The commitment to peace, stability and human rights at the heart of European foreign policy will pay off in the long run. This means addressing the causes of conflict and suffering, not just treating the symptoms.

What does the darkness of humanity look like? The documentation of the horror proves again and again how unworldly humanity is. Images and films have the ability to evoke emotions and tell stories that words alone often cannot convey. They show the cruel consequences of war and oppression in the world. They bring into focus the suffering that is often hidden behind political rhetoric and statistical data. Images of suffering children in crisis areas or scenes from war zones are often used as a shock tool to mobilize the public and draw attention to grievances. Despite the harrowing content, there is also a deeper message that often goes beyond the immediate suffering. Consciousness raising not only addresses the absence of humanity, but also the resilience of the human spirit. Stories of survivors who maintain hope and compassion despite extreme suffering show humanity's ability to rise above horror. The confrontation brings with it an ethical question: what responsibility do we have as spectators? People tend to consume the images without taking the necessary steps to change them. The darkness of horror may be overwhelming, but within it lies the potential for change and hope - if we are willing to act.

The European Union is deeply engaged in the game of global challenges, in particular by supporting civil society, regulating and preventing conflicts and strengthening democratic principles worldwide. Through a combination of financial and technical support, diplomatic engagement and the implementation of robust policy frameworks, Europe is helping to strengthen democracy and freedom. We are looking at a unique political and economic entity that has its own worldview and style of government that significantly influences international politics. The European approach to governance is based on values such as democracy, human rights, multilateralism and the rule of law and aims to promote stability, prosperity and cooperation both, within its borders and on the global stage.

This leads to a completely different scenario, namely that of international sport. It is one of the most important stages today. But no one can stay silent about it anymore. Sport and politics can no longer be separated if you don't want to let the individual degenerate into a creature that simply obeys, even if the minds at the top positions are sometimes plagued by ignorance. Athletes should not be forced not to have an opinion. They even feel an ethical obligation to think about what is happening in the world. Human dignity, social justice and world peace are issues that world sports organizations cannot ignore. Anyone who, in one way or another, turns sport into an element of selfish propaganda, is heavily complicit.

There comes a point when sport transcends its own hemisphere and influences events and feelings far beyond the confines of stadiums and arenas. Athletes are not just hamsters running around blindly on their wheels; they are influential figures who shape and are shaped by the world around them. Sport's intersection with social, political and cultural areas underscores its profound importance to our society. Athletes have unique visibility and influence, making them powerful agents of change. Your actions and statements can resonate with millions of people, spark discussions and inspire movements. This responsibility and potential for impact are increasingly being recognized by athletes themselves.

In recent years, international sport has been hit by numerous controversies and corruption scandals, revealing a worrying trend of ignorance or willful misconduct among leaders of major sports associations. This behavior, particularly when accompanied by a worrying affinity for authoritarian regimes, whether covering up verifiable doping scandals or conduct that violates international law, requires public scrutiny and accountability. Of particular concern is the propensity of sports organizations to align themselves with authoritarian regimes. This insidious problem permeates the highest levels of global sports organizations and manifests itself in a variety of ways - from the attribution of major events to financial scandals to the cover-up of critical information and facts. Such corruption undermines the integrity of sport and erodes public trust in these institutions. Sports associations must implement strict compliance policies and conduct regular audits to ensure compliance with ethical standards.

It is well known from numerous media reports, that top sports officials allow themselves to be coddled by dictators, accept gifts and bribes for questionable decisions and turn a deaf ear to crimes under international law. Will those among them who want nothing to do with it ever be held accountable? What happened to the legal principle "stupidity is no excuse"? Traditionally it means that ignorance is not an effective protection against being held responsible for one's own actions. For international sport, a code of ethics promotes fair play, anti-doping measures and respect for all participants. It helps ensuring that sporting events are conducted with integrity of the positive, not the negative.

So-called "independent athletes" cannot be so independent that they are unaware of the machinations of their governments. How are Ukrainian athletes or those taking part in the Olympic Games under the banner of a so-called "refugee team" supposed to compete against athletes from the countries of their tormentors? By accepting unscrupulous athletes, even without presenting a national flag, the aggressor state behind them and the instrumentalized athletes will not change at all their attitude. This must not happen, it is definitely not Olympic.

In an increasingly interconnected global landscape, the idea of an ethical world code in international relations has never been more relevant or necessary. And neither diplomacy, nor business, nor sport are excluded from it. This concept encompasses a set of universally accepted principles and standards, that guide the behavior of states and international actors. In international sport, an ethical world code should emphasize fair play, inclusiveness and the health and well-being of athletes. It would promote equal opportunities for all participants and ensure that competitions are free from doping, corruption and other forms of misconduct, including political misconduct. By adhering to these principles, the global sports community could preserve the integrity of sport and its role in promoting peace and unity among nations.

And last but not least, the question must be addressed: What are Europe's security policy ambitions? The EU was originally founded on the principles of economic cooperation and integration in order to prevent the recurrence of devastating conflicts such as the world wars. Security is one of the prerequisites of economic interdependence. The resurgence of war in Europe almost 70 years later, documented by the Russian invasion of Ukraine, has highlighted the weaknesses in the European security landscape.

This situation has led the EU to reassess its strategic priorities and improve its defense posture. The current geopolitical climate is characterized by strategic competition, hybrid threats and increased military buildup, requiring a robust response to protect the interests of the continent and its people. The framework of a new security strategy sets clear objectives for the EU to effectively advance its security. It begins with the central assessment of threats in order to improve the coherence of defensive measures and ends with the concrete intentions to defend oneself. It is clear that the EU's security aspirations are closely linked to its relationship with NATO. But should it be enough? What about the obligations of individual NATO members? The EU is increasingly involved in civil and military crisis management operations to address conflict and instability in its environment and beyond. As cyber threats become more common, cybersecurity measures are being taken to protect infrastructure, the economy and citizens. This includes initiatives to improve collaboration among all members and with external partners. The EU must also step up its counter-terrorism efforts by improving information sharing and implementing measures to prevent radicalization.

To achieve these goals, immense tasks must be overcome, including resource constraints and balancing the transatlantic relationship. As the EU develops its security and defense policy, it must address these complexities to build a more resilient and capable Union that can respond effectively to the diverse security threats of the 21st century. These ambitions can only be fulfilled by investing in defense capabilities, aligning policies, sharing intelligence and supporting EU institutions and initiatives. Ultimately, the success of the EU security strategy depends on the collective commitment of its members to advance the principles of common security and strategic autonomy.

There is no point in flooding the airwaves with information about various trouble spots in international relations, but turning a blind eye to the background would be a negligent underestimation of the dangers. Could global politics be heading for a period of incredible upheaval? The global balance of power is changing. As wealth disparities widen, so does the potential for unrest and political instability. Rising temperatures, extreme weather events and sea level rise are leading to widespread environmental destruction and resource scarcity. These changes are causing mass migration, food and water shortages and increased competition for resources, potentially triggering conflict and exacerbating existing political tensions.

Additionally, radical islamism has emerged over the past few decades as a significant threat to international security and stability. This ideology, often associated with extremist groups and terrorist activities, influences world politics Its impact spans regional conflicts, humanitarian crises, global security threats, and geopolitical tensions. Countries like Syria, Iraq, and Yemen have plunged into protracted civil wars and humanitarian disasters due to the influence of radical Islamist groups. The IS seized large parts of Syria and Iraq, leading to massive violence and displacement. In Africa groups such as Boko Haram in Nigeria and Al-Shabaab in Somalia destabilize entire regions, causing thousands of deaths and forcing millions to flee. Afghanistan and Pakistan have struggled for decades with radical Islamist insurgencies that heavily burden both state structures and civilian populations. Effectively combating this threat requires a comprehensive approach integrating military, political, economic, and societal measures.

Social movements committed to issues such as racial justice, gender equality and climate protection are gaining momentum around the world. While these movements advance positive change, they also highlight deep societal divisions and escalate into significant political upheaval. Political polarization is worsening in many democracies, weakening institutions and undermining public trust in governments. This polarization is often fueled by misinformation and the spread of extremist ideologies.

While it is difficult to predict the exact course of global politics, the convergence of geopolitical tensions, economic instability, technological risks, environmental challenges, social movements and health threats suggests that the mankind is indeed heading into a period of upheaval. Navigating this complex landscape requires strong international cooperation, adaptive governance and resilient societies. The ability of global leaders to effectively address these diverse challenges will determine whether the coming era will be one of conflict and chaos or of transformation and progress. Observing the patterns of recent major global crises, a discernible escalation ladder emerges, pointing towards a potentially turbulent future. From the persistent conflicts in the Middle East, exacerbated by the Islamic Republic of Iran's aggressive posturing, to Russia's assertive ambitions in Ukraine, and the looming challenge in the Pacific with China's aspirations for global supremacy, the signs of growing geopolitical instability are unmistakable. Adding to this are the internal flare-ups of extremism and irrationality within democratic nations, indicating a multifaceted crisis that spans both external and internal dimensions. The convergence of these threats foreshadows a gradual outbreak of a destructive global crisis.

What should be done about it, how can the line of danger be overcome? Through diplomatic engagement, economic diversification, strategic alliances and international cooperation, the global community can work to reduce the risks of significant upheaval and promote a more stable and balanced global order. To effectively counter the diverse threats, a comprehensive strategy that combines military readiness, economic resilience and technological advances is essential. This approach ensures that Europe can defend itself against immediate threats, sustain long-term economic growth and leverage cutting-edge technologies to maintain competitive advantages. Military preparedness will be a cornerstone of European security. This is not just about a capable and well-equipped military force, but also about the ability to respond quickly to different types of conflicts and crises. Investments in advanced military technologies such as drones, cyber capabilities and precision-guided munitions are intended to ensure that the armed forces are equipped to meet the demands of modern warfare.

A continuous training and the development of adaptable military doctrines are essential. This includes joint exercises with all European armed forces that improve interoperability and readiness for coalition operations. Effective logistics systems ensure that military units can be maintained even during longer deployments. This includes securing robust supply chains across Europe for essential materials and equipment. High-quality intelligence and surveillance capabilities are critical for threat detection and strategic planning. These include satellite reconnaissance, cyber intelligence and human intelligence operations.

And what about military threats from space, including the possible use of space-based weapons or capabilities to attack targets on earth? In the long term, the greatest theoretical threat to the vulnerability of the free world is to declare space a military battlefield, as already described by the author in *"POLITICS @ global world. intl"* *(ISBN 9783759706041)* with regard to the dominance ambitions of China and Russia. The potential of space-based weapons to escalate conflicts, to increase the risk of miscalculation and to undermine global security and stability underscores the ethical challenges. The militarization of space would result in the weaponization of critical satellite systems, communications networks and navigation services, endangering the security of populations around the world on an unprecedented scale. If such developments escalate into a space arms race, the balance of power between spacefaring nations will be extremely destabilized. The use of weapons that cause unnecessary suffering, indiscriminate harm or long-term environmental damage violates the principles of international humanitarian law. To address this threat, it is essential that the international community work together to adjust norms, rules and agreements to prevent the militarization of outer space and preserve its peaceful use for the benefit of all.

A blend of military readiness, economic resilience and technological advancements forms the foundation of a robust strategy to counter diverse threats. By maintaining a strong and adaptable military, building a resilient and diversified economy and staying at the forefront for technological innovation, Europe can effectively navigate the complexities of the modern threat landscape. This holistic approach not only enhances Europe's security but also fosters long-term stability and prosperity. The integration of these elements requires strategic foresight, sustained investment and a commitment to continuous improvement, ensuring that the free world is prepared for both current and future challenges. And the dynamism of a European Union will be maintained as long as the drive for innovation and optimization is not lost.

A united Europe can serve as a beacon of hope and a model for effective cooperation between different political entities. European integration has already achieved remarkable successes since its beginnings. The creation of the single market, freedom of movement and a common currency have brought unprecedented economic benefits and opportunities to millions of Europeans. However, the mission of European unity goes far beyond mere economic integration. The idea can be successful, if many people want it. The unity of the European continent secures the future. It embodies a strong symbol of co-creation and solidarity. The challenges we face – be it climate change, economic growth or geopolitical tensions – require shared solutions. As the world grapples with transnational issues like pandemics, climate change and technological disruption, the need for effective international cooperation has never been greater. A united Europe can serve as a powerful example of how diverse nations can work together to tackle shared problems. By demonstrating the benefits of pooled sovereignty, shared resources and collaborative decision-making, the European project can inspire similar efforts in other regions and on a global scale.

Europe is at a crossroads between whether it should develop a realistic self-image, that recognizes its own strengths and weaknesses, or whether it should completely neglect itself. At this point, Europe is still economically strong and culturally influential, but at the same time must face the geopolitical challenges posed by the emergence of other powers. To balance China's influence in the Far East, Europe could strengthen strategic partnerships with countries such as Japan, South

Korea, India and Australia. These countries have a common interest in maintaining their sovereignty and security in a dangerous environment. Europe could help to further deepen its economic relations with countries in Asia in order to create alternative trade routes to China. Free trade agreements and investments in infrastructure projects are helpful approaches. Europe can demonstrate its values and norms, such as human rights and environmental protection, to encourage like-minded partners. This normative force of Europeans should be heard in the international arena. In addition, strengthening Europe's defense capabilities is crucial, in order to be taken seriously on geopolitical issues. A common security strategy would strengthen the European position while boosting reputation and cooperation in more distant regions.

When governments come under pressure, authoritarian regimes in particular resort to aggressive, reactive behavior. They are forced to take a tougher stance in times of crisis in order to demonstrate strength and to gain domestic political support. The unpredictable behavior of individual leaders uses manipulated enemy images to distract from their own difficulties. It is crucial that the international community remains vigilant and strives to defuse aggressive tendencies.

Early intervention, dialogue and the promotion of stability are important steps to reduce the risk situation. A lack of specialist knowledge in international issues would otherwise lead to fears of counterproductive reactions. Arrangements with reliable alliance partners are an opportunity to find common interests for collective cooperation. Australia could establish itself as a stake of security in the Indo-Pacific. It would have a large number of supporting partners in its wake, such as Japan, South Korea or Indonesia. And then it will come down to the US-Australian alliance. A parallel axis could be formed between Canada and Australia, which would be secured by a back-up in the between Canada and Europe. Such constructions of strategic networks strengthen the existing universal community that stands up for law and freedom. Europe's indirect responsibility is emerging, a call of duty that Europe may not have originally wanted, but which it cannot ignore. The various loops of solidarity have already been laid out as soon as the USA strengthened strategic missile bases in Europe and at the same time expanded the capacities in Australia to investigate the Chinese nuclear force. But, economic measures would be more reassuring than military strengthening. It remains to be seen whether they will work, if powerful captains of industry repeatedly oppose them and block all measures.

It is no longer about the singular defense of Taiwan, Japan, South Korea, Australia, Ukraine and thus Europe. The civilizational war between world views has long been officially declared without a muzzle by the triangle Russia - Iran - China. The conflict has developed from a purely military to a more comprehensive dispute, for example in the area of the semiconductor industry, in the different ideas about social order and international order and the associated trade disputes. In addition to traditional military conflicts, hybrid warfare, cyberattacks and disinformation are becoming increasingly important. These methods are part of a broader strategy to gain influence and to destabilize opponents. The alternative model of the world of despotism relies on national isolation, the expansion of zones of influence and thus a division of power in the world. What new is about the methodology, apart from the ultra-destructive military technologies, is the definitive realization that war and peace cannot be presented in binary terms, but have built-in intermediary stages under the cover of publicity, such as information warfare and cyber warfare.

Do authoritarian regimes believe they are winning the information war? They use social media and other online platforms to suppress anti-authoritarian movements and hinder democratization processes. Fake news has been used to influence several elections, for example in the USA and Europe. When Sweden wanted to join NATO, Koran burnings were staged, whereupon Erdogan's Turkey blocked Sweden's accession to NATO. "Intelligent repression techniques" are increasingly supplementing traditional methods such as violence and imprisonment. Digital surveillance makes it possible to control the population more cheaply and less conspicuously than traditional methods. Europe is now truly waking up to the need to gain respect in order to defend itself against attacks of any kind of totalitarianism.

There is a growing awareness that China is pursuing its geopolitical goals not only through economic pressure, but also through political influence, technological control and subtle methods of influencing opinion. China uses its economic power to influence countries and companies. Through trade relationships, investments and loans, especially as part of the Belt and Road Initiative, China can put pressure on other states to support its political interests. However, reactions to this vary. Is it a marketing idea from Xi Jinping that, as commentators claim, is disguised as an infrastructure project? Some countries are aware of this and are trying to reduce their dependence on China, but economic ties often make this difficult.

China's behavior in the UN or in other international bodies and multilateral forums shows how it is massively expanding its positions through economic offers. There are increasing concerns that China is attempting to influence public opinion and policy decisions in other countries through these channels. Western democracies have recognized this and are responding by taking measures to check Chinese influence in their countries. However, authoritarian regimes do not think much of individual human rights and basic liberal values. Diplomats and observers at the UN repeatedly complain that the People's Republic is trying to rewrite the basic values of the world organization.

China's efforts to lead in key technologies such as 5G and artificial intelligence are also seen as part of a strategy to influence global standards and create dependencies. Those who have realized this are beginning to rethink their technological cooperation with China to protect their national security. Europe's strategy appears to be to work with China in the spirit of selective cooperation in areas of common interests such as climate change or global health, while at the same time upholding its own values. To achieve this, economic dependence should be reduced by opening up alternative markets and supply chains. Cooperation with the USA on security policy issues would have a positive effect, while taking an independent position in other areas. At the same time, European defense capabilities and, in some areas, a certain technological leadership would have to be expanded in order to be perceived as an independent actor.

Being too accommodating to geopolitical pressures can risk losing credibility at the international level. Partner countries would interpret a flexibility as weakness, which would result in less influence on multilateral decisions. Europe's strategy requires a correct interpretion and anticipation of complex geopolitical dynamics. Misinterpretations could lead to wrong strategic decisions that have long-term consequences. Giving in to what was seen as a temporary situation usually creates long-term geopolitical disadvantages.

In additiuon, the responsible use of social media is discussed. Secure communication platforms for the exchange of information would have to be set up in cooperation with evaluation agencies. The population should be supported through education in media literacy and the use of evaluations in critical thinking in order to arm themselves against disinformation and manipulative content. By increasing investment in research and innovation, Europe could strengthen its technological sovereignty and become less dependent on Chinese technologies.

The future of European unity hangs in a delicate balance that will either coalesce explosively or quickly disintegrate. The crucial question is, whether this unity will be imposed, or shaped through joint efforts by civil society and political leadership. Europe's strength and resilience will be tested in the coming years and it remains to be seen how effectively the available resources and inherent strengths will be used. The means available are diverse: historical experiences - in retrospect, the large structures have been the most successful , rational rethinking - the sciences provide sufficient analytical practices and the determined will to success - which is expressed in successful communication. The interaction of these elements will determine whether Europe overcomes its current challenges and emerges stronger. There will undoubtedly be obstacles along the way, but through its institutions, Europe has the power to build a more resilient, freedom-oriented future.

The world may be at the beginning of a new era. In this context. Europe plays its role not only as a continent with a rich historical tradition, but also as a pioneer in reshaping global political and social paradigms. But how is Europe shaping this transition to new horizons, and what significance does this have for the international community? Large segments of the political world are still deeply preoccupied with revisionist dreams and ideological legacies. Polarization is driven in part by political actors' instrumentalization of social divisions. But there is growing awareness that the human mind can deal with dissonance and respond with more than just polarization. Transitioning societal mindsets to new horizons requires courage, innovation and determination. With its competencies in the areas of sustainability, digitalization, multilateralism and inclusion, Europe can not only secure its own future, but also participate in the renewal of the global political landscape. When traditional structures are put to the test, Europe shows that change is not only necessary, but also possible. By breaking new ground and adapting to the challenges of the modern world, Europe has the potential to compete on the world stage.

Globalization has led to close economic interdependence, making it difficult for countries to sustain their economies during massive crises. International policies have failed to promote sustainable and resilient economies, increasing pressure on governments to take drastic measures such as lockdowns to mitigate the economic impact. Careful planning, transparent communication and comprehensive follow-up are crucial to maximizing the effectiveness of a lockdown while minimizing the negative impact on the economy and society. Ultimately, it is an instrument that not only contributes to risk reduction in crisis management, but also provides important lessons for the future. Carrying out a comprehensive analysis means checking the effectiveness of whether and how the set goals were achieved.

The courage to discuss content is therefore a prerequisite for moving forward and developing sustainable solutions. This includes the willingness to critically question every situation, to develop an openness to new, perhaps uncomfortable insights and to remain steadfast in the face of resistance and criticism. This requires strategic foresight and the willingness to take risks and explore new paths. This is the only way Europe can act on the international stage as a designer and not as a driver. The so-called "tipping point effect" has become a key concept in the current debate. It represents the profound changes that have shaped the international order in recent years. Europe must not only recognize these developments, but also consistently adapt its foreign and security policy. This means questioning old certainties and developing new, realistic approaches that meet the current challenges. It's not about sacrificing ideals, but rather reinforcing them with pragmatic measures.

The evaluation instrument not only serves as a means of reviewing and evaluating measures that have already been implemented, but also as a fundamental tool for strategic planning and adapting future policies. Particularly for Europe, which faces numerous global challenges, professional and continuous evaluation is essential in order to act effectively and efficiently. Through a learning-oriented attitude, the findings from evaluations can be better implemented into concrete improvement measures. In an environment of limited resources and increasing demands, this is particularly important in order to avoid superfluity and to derive the greatest possible benefit from investments in civilian and military capabilities.

The spread of misinformation is accelerated by social media. Algorithms often promote content that is emotionally charged or polarizing, regardless of its truthfulness. Such societies are often characterized by mistrust, insecurity and instability. In a society of lies where untruths, misinformation and deception prevail, the way information is perceived, processed and used has a profound impact on society. People in a society of lies often develop a general skepticism towards information because they don't know what to believe. This results in deep cynicism towards new proposals. In order to get out of this vicious circle, education, media literacy and a critical approach to information are essential. Only through a joint effort to communicate reality transparently can the way out of the society of lies be found.

Programs must be based on priorities. If there is no more freedom, i.e. everything is rigorously turned off, there will no longer be any space for social or medical care. A peace order without its defense is not possible. The triage, similar to that in medicine, of simply casually determining whether any state or national community is allowed to exist or not, should be prevented. If security is not given priority, everything else, as social justice, health and economic progress, becomes unimportant. The long-term consequences can be devastating.

Game changes are theoretically and practically possible in international relations. Similar to sport, this requires intelligence and authority. When political intelligence, authority and charisma are missing, things become difficult. Modern Europe will not arise all at once. A longer process may be more realistic, but there is an opportunity to advance preparation for disruption unexpectedly quickly.

In summary, crucial elements are the dismantling of party-apparatus thinking, the abolition of the horrible nationalism, the emphasis on performance and evaluation and large-scale regional restructuring always under the consideration of freedom, security and prosperity. Efficient strategies must not exclude anything, especially in defense. This is also about the dominant visibility of quality and sustainability. A Europe of relaxed cooperation is not enough, to be able to act as a unit. And there are still far too many hostile counterforces, that want to break the framework. If Europeans coordinate their efforts and work towards common goals, they can build a stronger and more resilient community.

It will require a collective effort, that emphasizes courage and foresight not only from leaders, but also from citizens who believe in the principles of a democratic EU. By working together, they can create a resilient society, capable of withstanding the pressures of extremism. A consciously intelligent EU policy is a profitable investment in a hopeful future for broad sections of the population. On the one hand, narrow thinking in world politics can lead to a lack of cooperation and solidarity, making it difficult to solve global problems such as poverty, climate change and conflict. In addition, it can also lead to protectionism and isolationism, hindering free trade and international exchange, which ultimately inhibits economic growth and development.

ABOUT THE AUTHOR

J-G Matuszek

Universities: Innsbruck, Perugia, Salzburg. Language sciences. Graduate interpreter, Master's degree. Political sciences, Empirical system sciences, International relations, Communication sciences, Philosophy, Doctorate. Postgraduate studies at various institutes: Marketing, Advertising-PR-CI, Management-Controlling, Innovation and Development Management. Licensed consultant.

Career: Journalism, High school teacher, translator and interpreter. Manager at multinational corporations. Management contracting in medium-sized companies. Consulting and coaching in marketi

ng, international management, and HR. Board member and director in several companies in Germany, Switzerland. Management in the field of certification of companies and organizations. Board member of the Foundation "Globility-Circle", Switzerland.

Guest lecturer at various universities and business schools. Author. Parallel-career as athlete, Austrian Taekwondo Federation President, High-tech collaborations for performance diagnostics/optimization in business and sports.

Books of the author

NEW VALUE ECONOMY - Manager quo vadis? ISBN 9783981263206
MANAGEMENT DER NACHHALTIGKEIT   ISBN 9783658022891
SPORT FÜR MANAGER   ISBN 9783658036379
MANAGEMENT DER POLITIK - EUROPA   ISBN 9783990108529
EUROPÄISCH DENKEN   ISBN 9783738625592
EUROPÄISCH HANDELN   ISBN 9783750414501
MANAGEMENT VERSUS SPIRITUALITÄT?   ISBN 9783854314501
RUF NACH DEM SINN   ISBN 9783748144199
MUT ZUM SINN   ISBN 9783750418943
KICKOFF ZUM SINN   ISBN 9783752690200
MANAGEMENT SET-UP   ISBN 9783751941884
DER MANAGER *Roman*   ISBN 9783752648911
REFLEXIONEN Lyrik   ISBN 9783752603866
DIE TAEKWONDO MATRIX   ISBN 9783754352571
THE TAEKWONDO MATRIX   **ISBN 9783754395394**
TAEKWONDO MATRIX - SPORT EFFIZIENZ   ISBN9783758307423
EVALUIEREN   ISBN 9783756228805
PSYCHE DER WELTGESCHICHTE   ISBN 9783757810108
POLITIK @ GLOBALE WELT . INTL   ISBN 9783758307942
POLITICS @ GLOBAL – WORLD . INTL   **ISBN 9783759706041**

Verlag: BoD • Books on Demand GmbH, In de
Tarpen 42, 22848 Norderstedt
Druck: Libri Plureos GmbH, Friedensallee 273,
22763 Hamburg
ISBN: 978-3-7597-8717-0